The 12 Trials of Attraction

CW00385005

THE INSTRUCTIONAL MANUAL

Dedicated to all my followers, supporters and Hypnotherapists embarking on this great voyage into the remarkable powers of the human mind- Jennie

Author Biography

Jennie Kitching ADPR SQHP –

A teacher of The Advanced Diploma in Hypnosis and A Master Hypnotist since 2003, Jennie was awarded her first training qualification in 1994. Since that time she has become a certified trainer of a variety of differing methodologies in the corporate and private sector (including Louise Hay, '*You Can Heal Your Life*', Susan Jeffers ('*Feel the Fear and Do It Anyway*'). Additional study, notably of the works published by John Cleese and Robin Skynner ('*Life and How to Survive It)*' enabled Jennie to incorporate the more personal aspects of self-improvement into the traditional corporate training arena (GKN, Dudley MBC, The Law Society, etc) designing and delivering bespoke courses such as Pre-Retirement and Women's Development. Jennie presents with humour and enthusiasm drawing on this extensive knowledge base. Now she writes, teaches, continues her private consultations and delivers this knowledge to as many people as possible! You can contact her at info@hiprocom.com.

Jennie Kitching also has the accolade of being a GHR Accredited Advanced Senior Hypnotherapist, one of only a few in the world and now teaches others to that level.

She loves swimming underwater, plays the Ukulele and is an avid Cosplay enthusiast.

IMAGINE YOU HAVE ALREADY READ THIS BOOK

With trial one you created some silence in your life, not just when you were alone and peaceful because that is just too easy – you did it in the face of the chaos and demands of everyday living and gave yourself a chance to think and to respond differently to the same circumstances, which is the true essence of change.

With trial two you began to bend your perception of reality and what is normal and real in your everyday life, thinking things have not always been this way and don't have to continue to be this way either and you freed yourself from influence from your environment more and more.

With trial three you realised what you actually have complete control over is your focus in the present moment though the world may like you to focus elsewhere, you could still be at work and focus on enjoyment or in pain and feel more relief. Your flexible focus is your malleable friend in creation.

With trial four you revealed a few home truths to yourself that perhaps it was not the world's fault that you didn't have what you wanted, perhaps underlying it all was a deep rooted fear that had not been revealed. You realised it is okay to still do things whilst having that protection in place, though it felt uncomfortable, which caused resistance to soften, as you proved to yourself how resourceful you are.

With trial five you recognised that you are not here alone. There are many others in your reality and no one can function properly without integrating with others. You cannot have a job without a boss or a business without customers, or be an actor without a script or a bricklayer without the factory full of folks that make those bricks. We all need each other and your perception of some began to switch from foes to co creator friends.

With trial six you actually put your order in for that which you wanted knowing that you have always been asking, so you are now conscious of how to do it properly for improved benefit.

With trial seven you realised that your insights have been blocked somewhat because you did not understand how your Higher Self was attempting communication with you and now you have ideas on how to provide more opportunity for that communication to come through.

With trial eight you recognised the necessity of accepting the reflected assessments of how well you are doing, or as we know them commonly to be, compliments. You learnt that these are valuable comments from the Universe to point out your strengths and that negative comments are just as useful as you assess their validity and discount or consider their truthfulness and usefulness.

With trial nine you cleaned up your everyday language and realised your language creates your world as your feelings about those thoughts impact on reality. It works both ways – your thoughts and feelings come from you out into the world to share with others and the thoughts and feelings of others (including advertisers and skilled marketers) come at you affecting your reality.

With trial ten you realised what you have been affirming to yourself for years and where that was not serving you, you created more positive affirmations to counter the negative effects and alter your vibration to a higher frequency.

With trial eleven you discovered that the essence of what you want is already accessible to you and you stopped distancing yourself from it by thinking how it might never come, rather, you looked for the feelings it engenders within you, realising you want this thing in order to feel better in some way, so you look to the essence of that feeling within your present environment.

With trial twelve you really understood that your feeling state is energetic – that being sad saps your energy and being happy invigorates you. Therefore you developed ways to top up those energy levels and boost your vibration and health with mechanisms to achieve and maintain a happy state more often and a switch to initiate when you so desperately need it most.

Imagine you have now completed all of the trials successfully and you are the creator of your universe, feels good doesn't it?

Let's begin.

Thank you for reading!

Amazon reviews are really important to future writing projects for independent authors. Please leave a review for me because I would love to hear your thoughts about this book.

If you would like to receive your **FREE** preview of my next book please **email** info@hiprocom.com.

Thank you!

AUTHOR BIOGRAPHY 3

IMAGINE YOU HAVE ALREADY READ THIS BOOK 4

THANK YOU FOR READING!......................................9

   HOW IT WORKED FOR ME 16

TRIAL ONE: THE CLOSE YOUR MOUTH & OPEN YOUR MIND
TRIAL 18

   "EVERYTHING COMES TO THOSE WHO WAIT" 18
   WHAT TO DO 18
   WHY TO DO IT 18
   HOW TO DO IT 19
   THIS TRIAL'S TIPS AND TRICKS 22
   COMPLEX CREATIVITY 22
   THE UNIVERSE DOES NOT SPEAK ENGLISH 23
   RESISTANCE 24
   RESPONSIBILITY OF CHOICE 25
   SOAP OPERAS AND FILMS ARE USEFUL! 26
   YOUR EMOTIONAL RESPONSE IS ASKING FOR YOU!........................27
   PLAYING WITH PERCEPTIONS.......................................28

TRIAL TWO: REALITY TESTING: MIRACLE MULTIPLIER TRIAL .29

   "DON'T YOU EVEN THINK ABOUT IT!" 29
   WHAT TO DO 29
   WHY TO DO IT 29
   HOW TO DO IT 30
   YOU WILL KNOW THAT YOU HAVE PASSED THIS TRIAL WHEN: 35
   THIS TRIAL'S TIPS AND TRICKS 35
   WE DO IT ALREADY...35
   THOUGHTS HIJACK 36
   ARE YOUR THOUGHTS YOUR OWN; ARE YOU SURE ABOUT THAT?.......37
   YOU ARE SPINNING AND YOU ARE VIBRATING NOW 38
   THE SCIENCE BIT..39
   RECOGNISING IT HAPPENS ANYWAY.................................39

TRIAL THREE: THE HOCUS POCUS OF FOCUS TRIAL 41

"YOU HEAR WHAT YOU WANT TO HEAR, DON'T YOU?!"................41
WHAT TO DO 41
WHY TO DO IT 41
HOW TO DO IT 42
YOU WILL KNOW THAT YOU HAVE PASSED THIS TRIAL WHEN: 42
THIS TRIAL'S TIPS AND TRICKS 43
WHAT WILL CHANGE FOR YOU? 43
WHICH THOUGHTS AND FEELINGS DOMINATE YOUR VIBRATION? 43
WHAT'S THIS VIBRATION THING ANYWAY? 46
VIBRATIONAL REALITY OR NORMALITY? 47
HOW YOUR VIBRATION CREATES YOUR REALITY 47

TRIAL FOUR: THE REVEAL & DEAL TRIAL 50

"THERE'S NONE SO BLIND AS THOSE WHO DON'T WANT TO SEE"........50
WHAT TO DO 50
WHY TO DO IT 50
HOW TO DO IT 51
YOU WILL KNOW THAT YOU HAVE PASSED THIS TRIAL WHEN: 51
THIS TRIAL'S TIPS AND TRICKS 52
REAL FEARS AND PHANTOM FEARS 52
THANK YOUR FEAR 52
THE BIG LIST OF FEARS..54
FEAR OF VULNERABILITY AND VISIBILITY..55
FEAR OF SACRIFICE 56
FEAR OF FAILURE 57
FEAR OF SEPARATION/LOSS/REJECTION...59
FEAR OF SUCCESS 60
FEAR OF RESPONSIBILITY..62
FEAR OF COMMITMENT 63
HOW TO DEAL WITH FEAR 65
THE DEAL 69

TRIAL FIVE: THE CO-CREATOR TRIAL 70

"IT'S ALL ME, ME, ME, ISN'T IT!"...70

WHAT TO DO 70
WHY TO DO IT 70
HOW TO DO IT 71
YOU WILL KNOW THAT YOU HAVE PASSED THIS TRIAL WHEN: 71
THIS TRIAL'S TIPS AND TRICKS 72
YOU, CREATOR, YOU! 72
MOVE ALONG NOW 72

TRIAL SIX: THE 'PUTTING YOUR ORDER IN' TRIAL **75**

"BE CAREFUL WHAT YOU WISH FOR, YOU JUST MIGHT GET IT!" 75
WHAT TO DO 75
WHY TO DO IT 75
HOW TO DO IT 75
YOU WILL KNOW THAT YOU HAVE PASSED THIS TRIAL WHEN: 79
THIS TRIAL'S TIPS AND TRICKS 80
ENVISION YOUR POSITION 80
YOU DON'T HAVE TIME? 82

TRIAL SEVEN: THE PLIGHT OF INSIGHT TRIAL **84**

"LISTEN UP, YOU'RE A LONG TIME DEAD!" 84
WHAT TO DO 84
WHY TO DO IT 84
HOW TO DO IT 85
YOU WILL KNOW THAT YOU HAVE PASSED THIS TRIAL WHEN: 85
THIS TRIAL'S TIPS AND TRICKS 86
WHY DOESN'T MY SOUL/SPIRIT/HIGHER SELF/JUST TELL
ME? 86
THINKING FOR YOURSELF AND THE VALUE OF SLEEP 87
YOUR WAKING BRAIN DOWNLOADING 87
WHERE DOES YOUR CONSCIOUSNESS GO WHEN YOU ARE ASLEEP? 88

TRIAL EIGHT: THE 'THANK YOU MAY I HAVE ANOTHER' TRIAL
....**89**

"HE WHO LAUGHS LAST, LAUGHS LONGEST" 89
WHAT TO DO 89

WHY TO DO IT 89
HOW TO DO IT 90
YOU WILL KNOW THAT YOU HAVE PASSED THIS TRIAL WHEN: 91
THIS TRIAL'S TIPS AND TRICKS 92

TRIAL NINE THE AMAZING PHRASING TRIAL..........................**94**

"YEAH, BUT, NOTHING: CAN'T OR WON'T?" 94
WHAT TO DO 94
WHY TO DO IT 94
HOW TO DO IT 95
YOU WILL KNOW THAT YOU HAVE PASSED THIS TRIAL WHEN: 95
THIS TRIAL'S TIPS AND TRICKS 96
LET ME JUST EXPLAIN WHAT WILL GO WRONG WHEN 96
THE YEAH, BUT FAIRY..98
CONTRASTS..100
HERE ARE SOME OTHERS TO NOTICE TOO 101
TWO **BIG** REASONS WHY POSITIVITY AND AFFIRMATIONS DON'T
WORK FOR YOU 104
REPEATEDLY, WITHOUT PASSION! 104

TRIAL TEN: CONFIRMING AFFIRMING TRIAL **106**

"YOU'RE YOUR OWN WORST ENEMY!" 106
WHAT TO DO 106
WHY TO DO IT 106
HOW TO DO IT 107
YOU WILL KNOW THAT YOU HAVE PASSED THIS TRIAL WHEN: 109
THIS TRIAL'S TIPS AND TRICKS 110
THE RESISTANCES..110
TRADITIONAL RESISTANCES..112
RECEIVING VERSUS RESISTING 113
WHERE IS THE PERSISTANT RESISTANCE?.........................114
HOW YOUR NEGATIVE EGO BLOCKS YOU 114
I'M RICH I'M RICH, I'M NOT I'M NOT! 115

TRIAL ELEVEN: 5 MINUTES TO FLIP IT TRIAL........................**117**

"Come and rub shoulders with me, so some of that rubs off!"
....117
What to Do 117
Why to Do It 117
How to Do It 118
You will know that you have passed this trial when: 118
THIS TRIAL'S TIPS AND TRICKS 119
THE FOCUS FIVE CHALLENGE..............................121
Working with Essence 123
Remember Resisting or Receiving 124
So, Where's My Sports Car?...................................124
What Serves You? 125

TRIAL TWELVE: THE HIGH VIBES TRIAL...............................127

"There's no such word as can't, aim for higher than the note
and you will get there!" 127
What to Do 127
Why to Do It 127
How to Do It 128
You will know that you have passed this trial when: 129
THIS TRIAL'S TIPS AND TRICKS 129
Is Happy Easy?..129
You are having a laugh! 130
RESONANCE EQUALS REALITY 135
Spaced Out 135
The Vibrational Scale 136
THE HIGHS AND THE LOWS 136
Raising your Resonance.......................................137
Know Thyself 139
Are you Visual? 140
Are you Auditory? 141
Are you Anything Else? 142
My way or the Highway.......................................142

THE DAY OF RECKONING - REMINDERS 143

TRIAL ONE..143
You will know that you have passed this trial when: 143
TRIAL TWO..144
You will know that you have passed this trial when: 144
TRIAL THREE 145
You will know that you have passed this trial when: 145
TRIAL FOUR 146
You will know that you have passed this trial when: 146
TRIAL FIVE..147
You will know that you have passed this trial when: 147
TRIAL SIX..148
You will know that you have passed this trial when: 148
TRIAL SEVEN 150
You will know that you have passed this trial when: 150
TRIAL EIGHT 151
You will know that you have passed this trial when: 151
TRIAL NINE...155
You will know that you have passed this trial when: 155
TRIAL TEN 156
You will know that you have passed this trial when: 156
TRIAL ELEVEN 158
You will know that you have passed this trial when: 158
TRIAL TWELVE 161
You will know that you have passed this trial when: 161

EPILOGUE...164

THANK YOU FOR READING!..169

How it Worked for Me

After many years working as a therapist and trainer and helping thousands of people I found myself seeing a pattern develop that would serve as a workbook to assist and remedy the techniques of working with The Law of Attraction.

I have been frustrated for many years with the Law of Attraction industry and have seen many well intentioned works come and go and have found that many of my clients had either no, or very little, success with these techniques, leading to frustration and disenchantment.   The principles and ideas seemed so full of promise and yet the practicality of applying them in daily life was lacking and the support insufficient.

In experiencing personal and business success with applying real Law of Attraction techniques to my own life and clients I have decided to put them altogether in this book so that you too can benefit from them and experience the uplifting and amazing results from, what I have personally developed and have named, the 12 trials.

The 12 trials have been put together after many years of trial and error working with various Law of Attraction techniques and incorporating other Universal Laws.

I have personally had success with these 12 trials and believe that when you commit to really wanting to improve your reality YOU will achieve hugely positive results in all aspects of life.

Whether you like it or not you are on the 12 trials everyday of your life! Most don't realise this and end up repeating the same old cycles year in year out. This book will help you to not only recognise the trials but succeed in them.

The Law of Attraction does not work in isolation. There is so much more you need to know that perhaps has not been revealed in the past. If you don't choose to learn it here, then life has its way of getting you to learn it the hard way. I really want to help you. I hope you accept this help and enjoy all of the joy and prosperity the Universe has to offer those who complete the 12 trials.

TRIAL ONE: THE CLOSE YOUR MOUTH & OPEN YOUR MIND TRIAL

"Everything comes to those who wait"

What to Do

Today you will practise shutting up! Don't tell anybody, keep it a secret. Just listen more and say less. Much less. Write down your experiences before you sleep.

Why to Do It

When you speak less you allow your Higher Self to communicate with you. You are creating the 'gap' where there is an opportunity not only to listen to what is being said or done, but also to hear your own true response within. We often call this our intuition or sixth sense. This trial will introduce you to releasing resistance as you realise what your true response is and how that differs from the response you give out to others.

How to Do It

Get yourself a notebook and pen to be used especially for these trials.

1 At the first opportunity upon waking, look into the mirror.

2 Now go beyond your judgments of your hair or your wrinkles or your nose, or whatever it is you would like to change; see your face 'at rest' without any expression. You are lessening your resistance about yourself.

3 Practise your 'interested' face. Maybe you raise your eyebrows slightly or tilt your head; perhaps adopting a slight smile – there you are!

You might not have seen this expression on your face often, because you have only shown yourself your tired or critical face in this bathroom mirror, so it is nice to be interested in yourself and what you are to accomplish today, isn't it? In fact, the next time something that you consider 'bad' happens you can go to the mirror and use this expression on yourself.

It is important to be genuine – nobody is requiring you to be false here; just to do something different to your usual or 'normal' response.

Now. This is the face, or more accurately, this is the expression you have adopted millions of times to others and will adopt today more and more, to give yourself time to close your mouth more so that your mind will open up a bit. People generally love talking about themselves and others so this is not as difficult as you might think` and you will be surprised how long you can go without having to offer opinion.

4 Yes, you are going to listen and watch and learn from everything that happens to you today, everything that comes your way or that you engage with, you shall find absolutely fascinating, as if the whole world exists merely for your acknowledgement and interest. You are going to say a lot less back, just the bare minimum. As a rough guide, you should be aiming to say probably fifty percent less than you usually say. Your key concept for today is 'ssshhhhhh, listen!'

This is so that you can begin to really focus on how you feel WITHOUT telling anyone. As soon as you tell someone, then your own perception of how you feel and if you are justified in feeling that way is affected by the other person you are interacting with. Now that is good if you want sympathy or to be cheered up etc and, fine if you do. Just be aware of seeking that support or engagement if you do.

You will know that you have passed this trial when:

You notice throughout the day that friends, family and work colleagues may say to you things like, 'you are quiet today'. **If NOBODY says this to you, or remarks on your changed behaviour, you have NOT passed this trial – repeat again tomorrow before moving on. If you have seen no one today then you will have noticed your thought processes changing as you listen to radio or watch television and you will be interested and curious rather than merely accepting.**

At the end of your successful trial day you will have at least a page full of realisations about events and conversations and new perceptions on the content of your day. This will open the gateway to communicating with your Higher Self, which currently creates your reality.

Complex Creativity

Until we shut up a bit more the mind merely perpetuates what has gone before with standard responses to avoid getting ourselves into trouble and also to avoid hurting others. It is as if there is safety in continuing to speak and run the same mental programs over and over again for there is comfort in routine, regime and continuity. There is also boredom too, however, because your inner self, or unconscious mind/Higher Self, delights and comes alive in matters of complexity, engaging your creativity – otherwise it sleeps.

Also though, know this. Your Higher Self communicates with you in whispers. Why is it that you pay attention to some things more than others? When you can sift and sort through all the obvious stuff that crowds your mind and then wonder why you are now focused on this particular thing rather than that ....

That's when you can follow your influences backwards and be interested in how your thoughts originated. Then you seek out coincidences, those incidents that keep occurring, coinciding with each other to get your attention.

THE UNIVERSE DOES NOT SPEAK ENGLISH

So, you may have heard or read that the Universe delivers to you that which you want. Yes, that's true. For any law to be a law, especially a Universal one cited in so many works by so many authors for so very long. It must be consistent, reliable and absolutely, without question, true.

It may be correct to say that the Universe brings to you that which you want, though not necessarily, what you ask for.

What you are asking for needs examination.

Resistance

You may have heard that creating your positive future is merely a task of getting rid of your resistance and all the good stuff will flow to you.

Until you know exactly how you are thinking and how those resistances are being demonstrated each and every day, this is an impossible task.

To become conscious of your thinking patterns you need to know a little about your brain and how your inner self interprets things.   Be told not to think of a pink elephant, you have to think of it and try to dismiss it. Try not to think about how your eyes automatically follow these very words on the page or how your chest rises and falls with every breath you take; tell a small child that whatever they do they must not smirk or giggle or so much as cough at a funeral and that is then all that is on their mind and it becomes very difficult not to cough as one imagines what that tickle in the back of the throat and the dryness in your mouth feels like.

Responsibility of Choice

Now, some things may have been said during today that you did not agree with and usually, when you were NOT closing your mouth and opening your mind, you would have put that right: you would have made sure that other person understood your point of view or even told them outright that they were wrong.

Now, however, you are closing your mouth more and opening your mind you can be aware of what you THOUGHT about what they said. Maybe someone insulted you even and you became a little off balance, upset, or disturbed and you wonder why they would say such a thing and what you did to deserve it.

In not responding in your usual way, you have more energy to devote to what is going on in your head and in your emotional response – and ultimately what is affecting your energy signature, or your vibration.

Therefore you can take responsibility back knowing it's your response, your ability to respond, to that stimuli which is actually causing the upset. That's the good news because when you realise it IS your response, you can change your response to it. Eventually you will be able to choose better feeling thoughts and focus all your attention upon that challenge until you feel better.

Soap Operas and Films are Useful!

Maybe you are bursting to comment on something on television; on a story in the news or a particularly stimulating show. One of the most useful elements of exaggerated soap operas and Films is that we can see the character develop and unfold of people we may never choose to encounter.

Maybe you can understand how one could be driven to insanity or murder or adultery now you have seemingly watched the entire life of a person unfold before yourself in less than two hours. You have seen their experience through their eyes and the varying perspectives of other characters sharing their world.

In fact, we are so capable of diving into someone else's reality that we often lose connection with our own as we listen to well-intentioned sympathetic advice from others who do not think in our heads, or feel in our bodies. The only one who really knows what is good for you, is you.

Your Emotional Response is Asking for You!

The Universe responds to what we are asking for, though it reads our vibration rather than what we think we are asking for. We need to learn to understand how we ask, because we ask all the time! We do not ask in words for the most part, but by our emotional response to our environment. Also, when we really need help from the Universe that seems to be the time we close down and lose connection with powers that can help us.

This is rather like being in a really bad mood and not wanting to watch a comedy show because strangely we want to stay in the bad mood. Shaking off resistance is imperative, as is asking for help when

we need it most and then allowing ourselves to
RECEIVE it too.

Playing with Perceptions

Play with perceiving people and situations differently.
Such as a fast sports car speeding past you… what
do you think of the driver, what COULD you think
instead? How COULD you think of your
partner/boss/neighbour differently? What could be
going on in their lives that you will just never know
about. By closing your mouth and opening your mind
more, you reconnect with your own opinions and
thought processes. You have lessened your
resistance by not engaging in dialogue with others
about your opinions and you have become curious in
what you are giving out to others and to the Universe
at large.   Well done.

TRIAL TWO: REALITY TESTING: MIRACLE MULTIPLIER TRIAL

"Don't you even THINK about it!"

What to Do

Today your trial is to evaluate what is REAL for you and what is illusory, what you are being positively AND negatively influenced by. You will engage with others to find the like-minded within your experience – you will be brave enough to find out who your friends are AND who you want your friends to be.

Why to Do It

Usually, we 'find out who our friends are' when we find ourselves in dire straits and desperately in need of that support and true friendship. At those times, that support that comes from sometimes the most unexpected source, can seem like a Miracle. You can save yourself half a lifetime of heartache by proactively learning one of life's hardest lessons within days. Are the thoughts you are having yours or somebody else's? What is 'normal' to you? When you recognise the influences that surround you, you can return to having control over your own thoughts and realise what is true for you; you begin to recognise what is real.

How to Do It

Now that you have experienced a little quiet time whilst being in the presence of others and you have written down how life was a little different yesterday, you are ready to face reality. Reality in these modern times includes your electronic world too. Social Media avenues, such as FaceBook, Twitter, LinkedIn etc, are now to be utilised much more effectively for you. 'That which is like unto itself is drawn'. Realise that those postings and remarks that irritate or bore you are there because you have attracted them. A fundamental principle of The Law of Attraction is 'setting your intention'. Announce to your world your intention by posting a message exactly thus, **'I AM DOING THE 12 TRIALS'**. As others respond and ask what you mean, this is an indicator that they are ready: the Universe has selected them to test your resolve. Your response to their enquiry must be to merely send the link to the book on Amazon and let the Universe do the rest. It is important to let go of the outcome: you are just doing the trials and now you are giving others in your reality the opportunity to join in - just send the link and let it be. Let the Miracles Multiply for you and for those who wish to play. Remember to use your notebook or jot memos down on your mobile phone for this trial too.

Today just be interested in how you think and form your opinions with or without interference or invitation from others. Notice how you feel about comments given to you and acknowledge the support and notice where it is lacking. Do not engage with any negative or lack of support, for that attention will draw more of the same to you. Just be interested then let it go. You are finding your network of supporting, helpful, encouraging friends; you are actively finding like-minded souls from every avenue available to you.

When others offer their opinion and statement about reality to you, you could merely repeat it back to them and be curious about where that came from. This is taking things further than yesterday's trial, for now you interact by commenting. You are an active participant in your very own version of reality and you are causing ripples of intention to flow forth from you to see what comes back. You can take this as far as you wish.

For example, you arrive at work and some mentions that it is a 'miserable' day, because it is raining. State (in a calm, even tone, which is important to do!) something like, "oh, it is a miserable day because it is raining, that's interesting" and note the response. The 'that's interesting' phrase is enough, though you may want to expand. Maybe someone says you look tired. "look tired, oh that's interesting." In doing this, you reiterate to yourself what influences you are being surrounded by. The person you are with may offer a range of reasons to back up what they have said and why they feel that way, or may just ignore you and walk away. Remember you are more interested in what YOU are thinking at the moment, rather than what they continue to say.

If you are pressured to give an opinion merely say that you will have a think about it and let them know later. They will forget. If it is truly important enough to them, they will ask later.

Maybe you are home alone, watching the television or listening to the radio and you hear the news and a reporter says that crime rates are rising, your response will be, 'Oh, crime rates are rising, that's interesting'.

You may see or hear an advert on television or radio, or on a billboard, telling you to vote a certain way, or buy a certain product that will improve life for you in some way. Did you know that this X brand washing powder will get your clothing much whiter than before, did you realise you can get nought percent finance on a new three piece suite or shiny new car and pay nothing for the first year? Your response will be, 'that's interesting'. By doing this you will find your Higher Self either agrees or disagrees with it being interesting. If it is interesting to you then you will know because you will have other thoughts connect to it.

You are surrounded by stimuli almost minute by minute in the busy environment of today's world. Your electronic world connects you around the world and around the corner, in seconds. It is easy today to find out who your friends are and you need not have the pain of waiting to find out in any other manner!

It is imperative that you do this trial WITHOUT judgment or blame as to whose fault it could have been that you end up in a bad mood, if that is the case. It is our own response to the stimuli that creates the mood. **Remember, YOU started it!** Stay in control of you.

This trial is to provoke REAL thought in your day, rather than falling back into old patterns of automatic responses.

You will see from your observations in your diary or journal that you are influenced, positively and negatively by your environment. You have a perception of what is normal and real for you and this can vary for others. This trial will help you to screen out the negative parts of your environment and only allow in the positive. See how many positives and how many negatives you have in just one day. Your Miracles are Multiplying.

You will know that you have passed this trial when:

You have genuinely been interested in the statements you have heard throughout the day and you have NOT responded automatically with your own opinion or your usual emotion. You have calmly, in a matter of fact manner, stated your intention and told your world who you are, what you are doing and given others the chance to join you. If you have been successful, congratulations and move on to the next trial, if not, repeat this trial tomorrow.

THIS TRIAL'S TIPS AND TRICKS

We Do It Already

Develop awareness of the prophesies you yourself make every day as to how life will work out for you and be curious about them eg 'if I don't do this, then THAT will happen...' 'If it is raining, then it is going to be a miserable day' etc. Realise how some of these are programs other people are running and may not be your own worries. Sometimes we are overly cautious about our beliefs and attitudes to save what we may think is a barrage of opposition or lack of support, or even teasing. Yet, often, we back up others in their particular beliefs in cloaked politeness or awkward agreement. To make the Law of Attraction work **positively** for you (because it IS ALWAYS working for you) you need to be clear and firm in your INTENTIONS AND ATTENTIONS. If you don't, it's no big deal, you will just continue to attract the stuff you say you did not want. Your unconscious is always listening.

THOUGHTS HIJACK

Where do your thoughts come from? What sparked off that idea? Many times it is from your environment. 'Are you really going to buy that?' Do you think you don't deserve? It may be okay to spend some money on someone else though selfish to do so for yourself? Maybe it is, maybe not. This is your perception which is based upon your upbringing and your wider environment, your belief system etc.

Are your thoughts your own; are you sure about that?

It is time to take your power back and RECOGNISE when your thoughts are hijacked and what you can do about it to return you to some sense of balance.

The first step is in the recognition that you're thinking about something in a particular way because something in your environment caused you to think that way. The way to return to balance is in awareness and noticing, "I don't feel good at the moment" It is actually your emotions which are your guidance system which will tell you and point you in the right direction of getting back on track.

So, when you don't feel particularly good find a way to feel good. Seek a way of thinking and feeling better thoughts and feelings so when you don't feel positive rather than ascertaining how that happened and who was responsible for implanting the negative thought etc, instead RECOGNISE that it is your reaction to the stimuli that's causing the anxiety.

You are spinning and you are vibrating now

It may not be working out exactly as you would like and that is because you are vibrating.   Right here, right now, you are vibrating. You are spinning too, of course.

You might already know that any point on the surface of the Earth is moving at 1675 km/h or 465 meters/second which equals 1,040 miles/hour. Just think, for every second, you're moving almost half a kilometre through space, and it never even messes up your hair.

Well, maybe now that you are remembering how fast you spin, by forces beyond your control, it may not be too much of a leap to recognise that you also vibrate. All life does. That is because all life is made up of energy.

The science bit

Without getting into too much of the science stuff, everything is made up of energy, of particles and molecules and protons and electrons, which is all moving.   By the way, the great news is, your Vibration IS under your control though you may not be aware of this fact yet and that's why this book is so crucial to your understanding and awareness and how you will be able to make some positive changes easily and quickly just like I have done for hundreds of clients and delegates over the years..

Recognising it happens anyway

So, we do it already; we create our own reality and this first step is RECOGNISING how it happens. You see, we do it alright, though we do it unconsciously, which of course means we do it without awareness. As the majority of our repetitive thoughts are unconscious, then we are not aware of thinking them so how can we catch them and turn our lives around I hear you cry. Well, you can tell what's been going on in your brain by how life is panning out for you.

Then we need to kind of back up and recognise what sorts of thoughts would lead to that kind of a reality.

It is then the magical REALISING comes in.   Please have a good think about this word. Realising means making real.   Now reality can differ from person to person according to perception so your reality really is YOUR reality. Really, it is.   Real….ising is the active participatory manifestation of your thoughts made real.   So, when you recognise and realise then the magic of changing those thoughts results in a changed reality. Now, you will begin to witness the Miracle Multiplier as THAT WHICH IS LIKE UNTO ITSELF IS DRAWN.

TRIAL THREE: THE HOCUS POCUS OF FOCUS TRIAL

"You hear what you WANT to hear, don't you?!"

What to Do

What you give your attention to expands.   Response attentiveness attracts similar thoughts and experiences and it's time to notice. Spend the entire day ONLY focused on the positive aspects of life.

Why to Do It

How you feel in any moment governs your thoughts and your actions. You may have lots of plans to improve yourself and your circumstances, but if you are not 'in the mood' they will not happen.   You may think that an ailment will cause you great pain or discomfort, so it does. The more you focus on relief, the more relief you feel. The more you focus on anything the more it becomes and the more you may think about *desperately* wanting something the more you may focus on the absence of it right now.

How to Do It

Find every positive in your life and focus on it, for example.

I am awake and the sun is shining with a warm glow or, it is raining, giving life to the plants and the trees.

I love the taste of my breakfast!

My car is so reliable!

My bed is so comfortable!

My family/friends are so supportive! etc.

You will know that you have passed this trial when:

In your notebook you have a list of at least twenty positive aspects to your day.

What will change for you?

You notice genuine smiles and the help you receive from others, or a kind comment or action. You see them written in your book. You connect positive focus with an enhanced life experience. You feel better and are less negatively affected by others and some people make more effort to convince you of how bad life is, or avoid you completely, whilst others comment positively to you and enjoy being with you more. You recognise that you create your reality by way of where your focus lies in any given moment.

Which thoughts and feelings dominate your vibration?

If you are 'usually' or more often than not, in a negative (angry, irritable, sad. lethargic – you give it a name!) mood at work/with that particular friend, during a telephone conversation with a particular person, or whenever you think of money, then stop it!

Tricky isn't it? Notice in the following paragraph how one thought can connect to many others and spiral downwards quickly. Thoughts gather momentum at the speed of light.

For example, it could be that you are feeling low about not having enough money. Therefore, your dominant vibration is one of lack. These thoughts and feelings about lack lead to feeling you are not appreciated at work, else they would pay you more, or that your spouse spends far too much of your money which you would like to spend on other things, causing you to resent the holiday plans because you shall have to work so hard to make the money back and not want to buy that new car so convince the family to put up with the rusting, unreliable one. Every bill that comes your way you feel you struggle to pay and you begin to get irritated with those who share you life and your home because they are wasting electricity etc. Maybe you have been disliking that job for some time and your unconscious is trying to influence you to start a business or get a new job that interests you and pays more.

In the above case you could step into feelings of dissatisfaction, which originate in the job you won't give up, but which get superimposed upon your relationship and suddenly nobody can please you, no matter what they do, you are just so hard to please!

You could instead feel unappreciated, which originates in the promotion you did not get, though shows up in you feeling that you are taken for granted by others and you emanate despondency.

There are many ways to allow negative vibrations to thrive in your vibration which ultimately come from a certain source to stimulate you to change - though can result in you refusing to do so and instead you may radiate out unhappiness.

Another example is that you do not feel you are loved enough and so your dominant vibration is one of lack too. Maybe thoughts come to your mind like, 'If you loved me, then you would….". Though of course you do not say, you are just gathering evidence that you are not loved. Maybe you and your partner have different criteria for giving love to another, one may think they are suffering terribly by staying at work long hours to get the overtime money whilst the other thinks 'if you loved me you would be home by now'.

Dissatisfaction, lack of appreciation, despondency, lack of deservability, feelings of loneliness can all result from the same root and actually have nothing to do with where they get expressed. Usually, we express them when they burst out because they NEED to be expressed, though they come out where you feel safe to express them - at the kids rather than the boss, for instance.

At this point, do not think about the source of your angst, just notice the angst!

What's this vibration thing anyway?

You give out an energy signature which is charged by your emotional state. This is what is constantly 'read' by the Universal forces and responded to consistently.

VIBRATIONAL REALITY OR NORMALITY?

This vibrational reality is PRESENT TENSE – so this is where dwelling on the past and blaming the parents really has no merit. The time is now. The power is now. If you are feeling despondent, your vibration is sending out that signal NOW to collect more of it.

Trouble is, manifested reality seems to get more kudos than your vibrational reality. We like the validation of others, of certainty, of our manifested reality so this is why we join self help groups and gather together in village halls to bemoan the unfairness of life, on the state of the local park/our misbehaving body that is growing increasingly fat/the inadequacies of the health services and save the trees foundation. There are some important points to bear in mind here.

How Your Vibration Creates Your Reality

1. Physical reality is a manifestation of an INTERNAL state [Universal Law of Correspondence]

2. You want what you want because you have an awareness of someone else having it, or being it, by comparing yourself and what you have with others that share the planet with you. When you are in a competitive state of mind you are disconnected from your own creativity and the originality of your own potential creations, looking to others to do it better than or just as good as, or worst of all, never being good enough. What is your state regarding that which you want? Competitive? Creative? [Universal Law of Relativity].

3. If your vibrational signature creates your reality, it is a good idea to clean up that vibration and begin to focus more and more on the positive aspects of your life experience DESPITE what negative things may be occurring in your life at this time. After all, these are just things that you perceive at this moment in time as being negative and may actually serve you in the long run.

Ultimately, all life experience has value and sometimes it is only by looking back on past experiences with a certain fondness (like the best days of your life were your schooldays, yes?) that this becomes clear. When you are eighty years old and looking back at photographs of yourself now, you will forget all the troubles with finances and relationships that you currently hold in focus: you will be focussing then on your now beautifully smooth skin and the sparkle in your eyes and the fact that you have all those years ahead of you to live life to the full – or not, it is your choice.

TRIAL FOUR: THE REVEAL & DEAL TRIAL

"There's none so blind as those who don't want to see"

What to Do

Acknowledge the fear, make a deal and move forward.

Why to Do It

The most common resistance that stops people from creating the good things in life and what holds everybody back is F E A R.   Your negative ego is more clever than you here, as it disguises the fear in plausible ways to hide it from you because it does not want change and it is frightened, therefore it makes you frightened.   Reveal and Deal with that fear and you move forward fast so hold onto your hat.

How to Do It

Use this trial to reveal and deal with the fear. Look at the list of fears here. Recognise what you are afraid of and know that there is a part of you that, in the guise of keeping you safe, sometimes resists things that are good for you. With each one in turn, write which do not apply; write which USED to apply and you have overcome and write which you might be in the midst of right now.

You will know that you have passed this trial when:

You have acknowledged the fear and you know which fear/s belongs to you and learn that your particular fear is there to serve you and keep you safe and now acknowledged, you rise above it and trust yourself to protect yourself in a new way, drawing upon all the resources that you have accumulated by living life up until now. You know you have passed this trial when you have felt the fear and have written in detail about doing the thing that you fear most and have given your story a positive outcome. Now visualise it and feel the success and relief in achievement knowing that the next time you face a situation of this sort you have a new way

forward that will lead you to overcoming rather than
succumbing.

THIS TRIAL'S TIPS AND TRICKS

Real Fears and Phantom Fears

You are born with two fears. Fear of falling, which is
passed on through your genes to stop you from
falling out of a tree and fear of loud noises in case
you are about to be attacked. Yes, fear of falling and
fear of loud noise are the fears inbred into you. All
others have been learned by you in this lifetime. You
have been on the lookout for danger since you were
born, it is important to your survival and thriving that
you pick up on them.

Thank your Fear

Fear shoots out adrenaline into your system giving a
burst of energy to the longest, strongest muscles in

the body to enable you to run away quickly or to stand your ground and fight.

This is good when we deem it necessary to have such heightened alertness, though is debilitating when we consciously think we should **not** be experiencing it (though our unconscious thinks it appropriate as it wants us to do something else instead!) and so we stuff it down and pretend we are okay giving presentations at work, for example, as we go through our personal hell. Some fears are completely illogical such as being terrified of some of the smallest and least harmful creatures on the planet and this throws our conscious and unconscious inner self into conflict as we choose not to be afraid and yet we continue to experience fear.

Go through the list that follows and have in mind, what the most prominent fear is for you. Once the fear is identified, move toward it in your mind. The fear will be just as real to your nervous system and to your body, so you will know when you have the right one/ones. Thoughts of that fear will connect to past experiences and link together to cause you to feel sad.

Often we want to protect ourselves, not from the thing that we fear, but from even feeling the fear! It may be better to face the fear, get it over with, realise we are still alive and know that we have released the power it had over us; released the resistance.

Experience the worst that could possibly happen, 'I'm afraid I will lose my job', ok, go lose your job. Get fired in the worst possible way. Plan out your approach then play it through the way you want it to be.

This only needs to be done in your head though, the mind really does not sense the difference, remember. As we do not usually want to face our fears, they can be cloaked in mystery and be difficult to understand. Understand at least which category your particular fear falls into and you are almost there.

The Big List of Fears

There is:-

Fear of vulnerability and visibility

This is the feeling of being vulnerable to attack, criticism and judgment. We may live our lives worried about what everyone else thinks of our behaviour and try our utmost to be 'good' and honest and true. We put others first and hide behind them, wanting to support them to be the best they can be as we stay in the shadows. We serve the world incredibly well, though let ourselves down.

Recognition: I become visible to myself when others bring to my attention, something I had not recognised. This sends me into a frenzy of whether or not I am doing the 'right thing' and then the 'right thing' seems different according to who I am speaking to. In wanting something, such as giving a speech at work, or seeking out a new relationship, I am forced to judge myself and my worthiness and I feel vulnerable and unprotected.

Strangely, the people who often have this fear have given themselves situations to deal with in life which mean them facing that fear continually in the hope of overcoming it – therefore some of the world's top performers vomit before every performance and some of the most attractive and loveable people fail to initiate relationships.

This fear is applied in presentation anxiety, performance anxiety, initiation of relationship (dating) worry etc.

When you know you are 'over it'

Insults just bounce off you as you know they are not true and say more about the person giving them than they do about you. You no longer get 'stage fright' and if you go to an interview or give a presentation at work, you are just as interested in them as they seem to be in you. Life returns to balance.

Fear of sacrifice

This is the fear of thinking that if you do this or get that then there will be something that you shall have to sacrifice. You ask, 'what shall I have to give up?' This is surely too good to be true, so if I get the job maybe I won't have enough free time. If I enter into a relationship, what will I have to do for them and how will I have to be different?   What shall I have to become?

This fear is applied in commitment issues, changes of employment, retirement anxieties, parenthood etc.

When you know you are 'over it'

You are concerned about the sacrifice, but you go for it anyway: you get another job, you have a child, you get the pet that needs looking after and even though, yes, there is time and effort involved you find yourself enjoying your new status and are so glad you did it.

Fear of Failure

This is the fear of not getting it right, of failing, of losing. What if you might not achieve it! Everyone will know (there is a link to the fear of visibility)   You find yourself thinking, 'I would hate to feel like I did it wrong, like a loser, like a failure', so you don't try, preferring to think that you don't want it anyway; you prefer not to feel anything rather than to be a failure. You take it personally, you put this thing, this action, this ability at the identity level - rather than thinking you have failed at something, you think of your whole self as a failure.

This is applied in blocks to change, eg change of job, change of status/relationship, blocks to dieting (or becoming more attractive), pursuing lifelong dreams etc. In this fear you stop before you even start, though you talk about it a lot and it frustrates others who try to tell you of your competency though you seem not to listen. This is the fear of the wishful thinker.

When you know you are 'over it'

You realise you really want something and are prepared to go for it. You change your job and realise the previous one was better and put it down to experience. You learn a foreign language and are laughed at for getting it really wrong and find yourself laughing at yourself too. You start the day deciding you are dieting and end up having a huge meal, thinking, oh well, I will eat less tomorrow, never mind.

Fear of separation/loss/rejection

This is the fear of having something valuable and thinking you will have the constant worry of loss. What if I lose it? What if I have it and love it and appreciate it and life is so much better and then it is stolen from me? Will I be sorrier for having had it? Better to have loved and lost? No way, for me, it is better to not have loved at all. The base fear of all fears is loss. You might not realise that you are frightened of losing something but you are and until that is acknowledged it has power over you. We are motivated by moving towards something lovely or away from something horrid, releasing the horrid leaves only the lovely and that's a good thing.

This fear is applied in blocks to beginning new relationships, procrastination in starting the novel, beginning the course of study, re-establishing contact with loved ones etc. You play out entire scenarios in your mind rather than taking action. In these scenarios you cannot accept that things might turn out well for you and the pain of the imagined rejection is overwhelming.

When you know you are 'over it'

You ask for that date or that promotion because 'what have I got to lose anyway, they can only say no'. When you get the 'no' then you feel relief, because at least you now know rather than the turmoil of indecision and 'what if' that has followed you for so long. Finally, you can move along and give something else a go and look forward to the time of acceptance instead, for it will be all the more valuable for the separations and rejections gone before, finally, you will have something of great value that is meant to be for you.

Fear of success

This is the fear of success, worrying that the actual having of something will not bring the promised joy you think it might. What if it isn't wonderful enough? What if the looking forward to it was better? I would have nothing to look forward to when I have it. What if it wouldn't REALLY matter? What if it is not enough? What if friends and family regarded me differently and I don't get the sympathy for my present position any more? What if they think, 'it's alright for you, but…' (links to separation fear). What if I cannot handle it and the pressure to continue to be successful just gets too much?

This is applied in the 'one hit wonder' scenarios of hit records and bouts of good luck. This is why some lottery winners get rid of the money so quickly to return to 'normal' because the anxiety of the new status was so uncomfortable.

When you know you are 'over it'

You accept the envy and even ridicule of your peers who wonder how you got so lucky or what did you do to deserve it. You can offer gifts and money without worrying you are humiliating another or belittling them, allowing them to refuse if they want, but knowing you want to help. You know that you deserve, yet so does everyone in their way. You know that 'normal' is a constantly changing state for everyone and you do not fight it. You are comfortable with change – with changes of behaviour in yourself and from others and are genuinely happy with your good fortune and willing to share.

Fear of responsibility

This is the fear of responsibility (which corresponds to sacrifice too). You choose not to develop rapport with creating your own reality. 'You mean, really, I created this? Why on earth would I create such a thing! Explain that one to me why don't you.' You do not recognise that creating aspects of your reality may be to understand something valuable about life that you yourself have asked for. 'I really do not understand how anybody could do that, how could they, why would they?' By being judgmental of others you are putting out thoughts of wanting to understand their experience and therefore drawing such experience to yourself and often bemoaning your bad luck, choosing not to recognise any link or coincidence. You have thoughts such as it is all their fault, not mine, if it were not for them I would be successful but I have to…. Etc.

This fear is applied in putting it all down to fate. It is what it is and that's that. Over zealous religious beliefs and the long term employee who had chances of other opportunities that may have served them better, becoming pregnant accidentally, looking through medical books to find what illness matches certain ailments and being relieved when the diagnosis is 'true' and staying too long in an abusive relationship or with overbearing parents. The fear manifests in the addict who blames the product for being in control of them and not attempting to stop, the one who moans about politics in the pub but never votes etc.

When you know you are 'over it'

You accept that whatever is happening to you may in some way be a result of your own involvement somehow, even if it is unconscious. You attempt to quit smoking/overeating etc. You know that even though the cards might be stacked against you, you can give it all you have and have a chance at changing things. You listen to sooth sayers and know that life can be different for you even if you are not sure how. You go it alone, knowing someone will follow or you learn to trust yourself to get by, whatever might happen, you will do your best. You stop blaming others or your environment.

Fear of commitment

This is the fear of commitment, taking a stand, some people may not like you. If you often feel caught up in the middle of an argument and trying to keep the peace and be friends with everyone, this may be yours. This is the sitting on the fence attitude that seeks to keep harmony and ultimately results in frustrations when others need to know whose side you are ultimately on so they know if you are friend or foe. This is the worry of letting others know your true feelings because if they do, boy, there will be trouble. This is the eternal batchelor or spinster who has opportunities at long term relationships and just cannot commit for there may be something better around the corner.

This is active in the compulsive date-goer who finds all sorts of things wrong with each boyfriend/girlfriend rather than taking a chance and moving in together. This is the one who flits from job to job trying to find the perfect one. This is the one everyone likes, but not too much and never too long.

When you know you are 'over it'

You speak your mind, do your stuff and some don't like it and that's fine. You lose fair-weather friends and gain lifelong companions.

How to deal with fear

To deal with fear, your aim is to shift the focus from what you worry will most likely happen and balance it with, equally, something else that might happen instead.   Everything has its antidote and you balance out negative with positive.   No one can tell you that your dreaded fear will NOT happen but you gain confidence that EVEN IF the worst happens and your fear comes true, rather than sinking into self righteous 'I told you so' that you will pick yourself up, dust yourself off, seek out that support you need and carry on, wiser for the experience.

I will give some examples I have come across to help you answer these questions. What I would like you to do, is to complete the questions that follow, filling in your own answers as they apply to you.

Fear of vulnerability and visibility: a) when I am slim men might make passes at me and I don't want that. Women who liked me bigger may start to see me as a rival. b)when I am rich I shall want to move into a bigger house and that will mean I shall have to explain how I got the money and why didn't I help my family out when they were struggling so?

I have a fear of being visible yes/no

I have a fear of being vulnerable yes/no

Fear of being visible to oneself when others bring to your attention, something you had not recognised or wanted to ignore.

I have a fear of being told

....

Fear of sacrifice, what will you have to give up? What will you have to become?

If I were slim/rich/pregnant/successful, I will lose

....

Fear of Failure – you might not achieve it! Everyone will know (visibility). I would hate to feel I had tried so hard and failed, so if I would hate to feel that, then I choose not to try.

I hate to fail yes/no

If I don't get it right I will keep on trying yes/no

Fear of separation/loss – what if I lose it? What if I achieve this precious, so sought after state of being slim/loved/rich and it goes? It would be like perfection was stolen from me. Would I lose it and be sorrier for even trying?   Like all those times I tried really hard, lost weight and put it all (and more) back on again. Like my friend who lost her husband and ended up in a Home?

I have a fear of failure yes/no

I have a fear of losing

....

Fear of success – what if it isn't wonderful enough?   What if the looking forward to it is better than actually being slim?   What if all my problems didn't magically go away? What if it is not enough?

I have a fear of getting

....

Fear of responsibility – if I do this thing, if I achieve this state of near perfection then I will attract others to me. I don't know if I would like to be surrounded by slim/rich people for they are not the same as me. This fear corresponds to sacrifice. A desire not to develop rapport

I love/hate being responsible

My true responsibilities are

....

Fear of commitment, taking a stand, some people may not like you.

I like people to like me yes/no

It's okay for some people to not like me yes/no

People disagree and that is okay yes/no

In understanding the fear and recognising it merely as a protection mechanism, you are then seeking out other things that matter: flawlessly elegant moments of joy and peace, exhilaration, serenity and timelessness, exquisite moments (not perfect, not ever needing to be perfect) good times, light and defining moments to focus upon. Without fear, without risk, life is safe, yes, though characterless and dull. The highs and lows of life are energising, rejuvenating and exhilarating.

It is time to focus upon pleasant memories from childhood, adolescence, adulthood – timeless times that MATTER. It seems when we turn into adults we begin to feel sorry for ourselves when we were children, and yet the child we were just got on with things and did not really sink into the self pity we can have when we look back nostalgically. There are always good times in childhood, we just seem to filter a lot of them out. It is a crying shame that some brilliant, wonderful experiences get lost from consciousness, remember them and make them matter again – so that mattering is present and alive – times that TRULY matter to you, you can reawaken them. Fear builds as safety becomes an adult focus, not just safety for the self but safety of the family unit and keeping out of harm's way. Though harm may not be the outgrowth of risk and balancing safety and excitement is everything.

The Deal

There have been events and circumstances when you felt the presence of your very soul/Higher Self calling you to be all you can be, someone better, the urge to become your best possible version of yourself. These are the times when your fear is felt the most and the opportunity to feel the fear and move on with the moment arises to challenge, to encourage, to evolve your life experience. Choose to experience the fear and move beyond it just to surprise yourself at how resourceful you can be, or don't. Maybe you are not ready. Opportunities do not but knock once, they keep on coming. Though do not dwell and remain in fear – instead, choose.

TRIAL FIVE: THE CO-CREATOR TRIAL

"It's all me, me, me, isn't it!"

What to Do

Make a list of the top three defining moments/events in your life that you have unconsciously and consciously created, good or bad! Write down who else was involved in these events, who helped purposely or inadvertently. What coincidences had to line up to make these happen?

Why to Do It

Taking responsibility for your participation (consciously OR unconsciously) in what you have in life points you in the direction of creating other things that you currently want and have stopped yourself from having. Knowing also, that nobody creates

ALONE and that everyone is a CO-creator is imperative too.

How to Do It

First of all notice where you are in relation to where you want to be. Write down the things, the top three life events that, at one time, you had no way of knowing how they occur in your life, yet happened for you.

You will know that you have passed this trial when:

You write your three stories of the defining moments/events and how these involved others and how they responded to, and co-created your situation, even if you do not particularly like the people concerned or they are no longer around for you. You find yourself writing detail, such as what you are wearing and what the weather was like during these events.

You, Creator, You!

You are already a creator, however you do not do it alone. Acknowledge how and what you have already created in order to manage how you may create differently, though do not dwell there. Selectively sift through your experience and recognise and focus on positives. Strangely, almost as soon as we manifest that which we want we almost discount the potency of that as we go after the next thing that we want. [Law of Vibration] This means that we stop appreciating that which has already manifested and it is important to count one's blessings and look for the detail in that experience.

Move along now

It is vitally important to take the learnings from your experiences and use their value in the present moment. We don't though, most often. We blame people and events and faceless corporations.

As you move through these trials you will have the tools you need to create your most positive of futures and you are not alone. You never were alone and you will never be alone. However, you can foster that illusion of loneliness if you wish and keep negative imprints alive. It is in the knowing that we need others in our lives that we can feel such pain when they are gone and also look back on events that were perceived as negative at the time they happened, creating them with wistful reminiscences in the now. Either way, bringing pain and loss into the present moment is to be avoided.

The problem is not whether you need a new job, whether your wife or your husband has gone or left, or that your parents did right or wrong, or that YOU did right or wrong, or the terrible things that occurred in your life should not have happened. It is not any of those things at all. It is your reaction to them. It is the add on sentences you say in your head, that follow such statements of fact, such as, "Oh, my father is gone! I cannot live without him!" Or, "I've got a terrible pain in my back! I'll never live a normal life again!" You will be learning how to turn these around soon in this book.

That is really the problem for when you give yourself those negative thoughts, then you are bound to feel depressed so you have to learn how to turn those sentences around, turn them around completely: "OK, so I made a mistake, but I have learnt from you and that sure as heck will not happen again" Or, "OK, so I miss my spouse/child/lover but I can start over using everything my life with them taught me." Whatever it is that you say to yourself about those past things you can be thankful to have others to share this world with and we all co-create together.

TRIAL SIX: THE 'PUTTING YOUR ORDER IN' TRIAL

"Be careful what you wish for, you just might get it!"

What to Do

Decide and write down, in detail, what it is that you want right now and the reasons why you want it.

Why to Do It

That which is like unto itself is drawn and you always get what you want in life, though not necessarily what is asked for, remember.

How to Do It

Let's begin with an example of what many people create in their work lives. Even though this example is about work, this trial can be whatever your focus is upon; a relationship, health, family, home etc. Notice that in these examples, it is clear that one needs to be careful what it is that we actually want and the reasons for wanting it.

Stage one- Got to get a job

I am inexperienced so this means I must accept a job with low pay and it may not necessarily be something I enjoy doing, though it will give me money and with it the power to buy things for myself and choice to do things that I want to do.

Notice that you excitedly found a job to do this for you and, at that time, you were fulfilled and pleased with what you had created.

Stage two – Had the job for a while

I have been doing my *unfulfilling job* for a number of years and if I *work harder* and *put more hours in* and take on *more responsibility*, I can get *more money*.

I *worked hard* and got promoted and discovered that the *job is still unfulfilling* and the *more money* is not really worth the extra *responsibility* and *more hours I put in*.

Notice that the italicised words (commands) are exactly the same.

Stage three – I don't want to do this job anymore

I *am overwhelmed by bills* so I *stay here* in this job that I hate and at *my age* I do not think I will be able to get another job and I *am too old* to start my own business. I have *lots of good ideas* about how I would like to be *doing things I enjoy but cannot* because I have to work instead. I wish the day would *go more quickly* because I do not like what I do.

I *stayed here,* and I feel *overwhelmed by bills* and *too old* and had *lots of good ideas* and the *days go so quickly* and I do not *like what I do though I cannot be doing the things I enjoy.* It's nearly Christmas yet again and the days just seem to *go more quickly* nowadays.

Notice that the italicised words (commands) are exactly the same.

1.Develop awareness of the prophesies you make every day. In the above example, we could change the three stages to:

Stage One Got to get a job

I am young and enthusiastic and I want a job that will allow me to be creative and fulfilled with good pay.

Stage Two Had the job for a while

I am unfulfilled in my current job so there must be something else for me that I find interesting and fulfilling and is well paid. I set out to find a new job.

Stage Three I don't want to do this job any more

I *left my unfulfilling job,* and I feel *eager to* use my *good ideas.* I am going to create my own business using all my abilities and talents and experience that I have gained over the years so that I *can be doing more of what I enjoy.*

2. Notice that we are ALWAYS creating what we want in life. Our actions, in inactions, are based on what we believe to be true for ourselves. When we find that we would desperately prefer life to be different in some important way this is our Higher Self's way of encouraging us to make that change. We often find we are talking ourselves out of it, or allowing others to, if we think it may be tricky or inadvisable to make the necessary changes.

3. Sit down and really think about what you WANT to happen in your life and create a picture, a feeling, a sound, a vibration about it. This is 'anchoring' the scene into your present day reality. You are making things tangible now, what would you smell? What would you see, what colour would this be? What sounds would be there? Who would say what? This, remember, is not really about a job in the example given. This is about fulfilment and using one's time and abilities in a way that is productive and gets those bills paid. After all, the bills will still be there if the work we do is fulfilling, or not.

Allow it to be real for you so your Higher Self listens.

4. Really feel what would be different in you and around you when this manifests. Know that anything is possible. How would others react? Write all this down so you can compare when it materialises.

You will know that you have passed this trial when:

You will have a clear and detailed description of that which you wish to have created for you in your life and what you wish to experience into your future. There are varied and different possibilities of exactly how these can occur and you focus only on that which you want not on how it will come to you.

THIS TRIAL'S TIPS AND TRICKS

ENVISION YOUR POSITION

Noting your position and sensing how you want things to be is an important matter. Allowing your imagination to skip and dance in the landscape of your envisioned preferred reality is vital. This is necessary to counter what one usually does when one reaches adulthood – which is continually worry about what IS wrong and needs improvement (thus creating more of the same). Understand that the reason we are so good at imagining what IS or COULD go badly wrong is our way of preparing for the worst and protecting ourselves. Therefore, because we do that naturally, it is IMPERATIVE that we also take some time to counter this with imagining what we DO want – just like when we were children and young adults and wanted to change the world.

Now, what are the steps of getting there? The steps to getting yourself into the vibe of writing and describing in detail what you want and allowing it to be present on the empty page are easy, honestly. You may have forgotten. You write about QUALITIES of BEING there (we will talk of essence later). Be there, enjoy, really, enjoy and make your imagination and dreams such that you are quite shocked when you 'snap out of it' that the physical reality has not caught up yet! You are exercising your imaginative creative muscle more consciously. You do it anyway, every night whilst you sleep, by the way. You do it consciously when you are awake by worrying about stuff. Time to put some of that energy to what you DO want rather than what you DON'T want.

You are just noting your position that's all.   Now. Rather than becoming swept up in what IS right now, focus on how you would like things to be in the future and also WHAT HAPPENS NEXT? We mostly fall down on our manifesting by falling into the 'happily ever after' trap.   You can be surprised at how things turned out, looking back, so be surprised looking forward and stop trying to apply logic and reason because you do not know how the Universe will line things up for you – that is NOT your job. Though you can wonder and speculate and be even more surprised when it manifests.

You don't have time?

Doing what you enjoy does not need time apportioned to it, you just do it because you enjoy doing it, so if you think you do not have time to do something, then that's probably not for you anyway. Replace time with intensity and duration with durability, find ways to make yourself vibrate at the same level as that which you want by choosing experiences, feelings and thoughts that resonate on the same level. The challenge is that we often do not recognise where life is working out really well for us. For example you want to be abundant about money, FEEL your abundance about your good health, whilst focusing on money flowing to you.

It is time for what you actually want and what you actually ask for to marry up: what you want and what you ask for need to equalise without your negative ego stopping it happening for you.

TRIAL SEVEN: THE PLIGHT OF INSIGHT TRIAL

"Listen up, you're a long time dead!"

What to Do

Ask yourself today, continually, 'How is my inner self communicating with me? What am I inspired by today?' Write down your dreams, your inspirations and all coincidences and observations.

Why to Do It

If you are not recognising the feedback you are getting, you stop listening, stop believing and ultimately shut down. Your Higher Self gives up on you, concentrating instead on other versions of you that are still paying attention and questioning life. Knowing your own particular way of communicating with your inner self is imperative to your success in life.

How to Do It

Find out where your inspiration occurs. When you have not been stimulated by outer sources such as television, internet and others, how do you feel and what is on your mind?

If you suddenly have a good idea or want an ice cream for no apparent reason, or a song just pops into your head, then that will most likely be from your inner self.

You will know that you have passed this trial when:

You will know the importance of writing things down on waking, you will have an idea just pop into your head, you will react differently to tv shows and chance encounters. You will have a list of coincidences, inspirations and dreams and you will have recognised what you are particularly drawn to that sparks your creativity and invigorates you.

WHY DOESN'T MY SOUL/SPIRIT/HIGHER SELF/JUST TELL ME?

If you get irritated (and who doesn't?!) at the manner in which your inner self communicates, or tries to communicate, with you then there is good reason why it does so in cloaked, metaphoric symbology. Some people have a strong urge to open a book, any book, and look at a certain page and read a sentence and find it applies to something they are dealing with. Others look to tarot cards,or roll dice.

We have cut ourselves off from many of the avenues through which this communication used to happen and are so busy and stressed within the barrage of information and data being thrown at us this way and that, that it has become difficult to think clearly. It may be difficult, though not impossible.

Thinking for Yourself and the Value of Sleep

Remembering the earlier trials, such as acknowledging where your thoughts come from, realise that on waking your thoughts are your own.

 Think about that then. Where do your thoughts originate as soon as you awaken?

The unconscious mind is completely in charge when you are fast asleep in bed at night.

Your Waking Brain Downloading

When you wake up in the morning, it is as if in that waking you get a download of information, of consciousness, as you become aware of where you are, who you are, who you are with.

At that moment as you are waking, and many people wake up just before the alarm, you may be wondering what the time is and there is a remnant of a dream somewhere, you know who you are, your name etc and that is your consciousness coming back in. That does not mean that the unconsciousness goes somewhere when you are awake, it has far too many tasks to do for you like that blinking that you are doing right now.

Where does your consciousness go when you are asleep?

Your conscious mind certainly goes somewhere when you sleep, as we can tell now by all kinds of equipment measuring brain wave activity, though your unconscious remains. It stays with you the whole time.   It still tries to tell you about that dream during the day when you are far too busy to listen!

TRIAL EIGHT: THE 'THANK YOU MAY I HAVE ANOTHER' TRIAL

"He who laughs last, laughs longest"

What to Do

Write ten positive aspects about yourself. Also, if someone gives you a compliment, add this to the list too.

Why to Do It

Until you can honestly take a compliment on the chin, not believing that this person is either wrong, or wants something from you; and until you can look at your own face and body without chastising it for not being perfect, you are holding negative influences in your vibration.   Negative influences in your vibration attract uncomplimentary comments and even insults from others and so having a negative self image becomes a self fulfilling prophecy as if you don't like you then others begin not to like you either.

How to Do It

Settle yourself in a place where you are comfortable and will not be disturbed and look into the mirror for five whole minutes (which is longer than you think, so time it!). Now say ten positive statements about yourself aloud whilst looking into your eyes and sense what your true response is and how true you believe these statements to be. Don't DO anything with these responses, just make a note and be interested. If you feel emotional, you are doing it correctly.

PLUS, today, look out for compliments.

Ask someone what they think of you, or what they think of something you have achieved and notice how you feel when they say nice things!

Stand in front of the mirror and say some positive things about who you are and what you look like. If you struggle a little, pretend you are someone who loves you very much, whether they are alive or dead, the love is still vibrant. Imagine it is they (your mother, grandparent, father, sister, child or other) who is saying these things. Realise in your non acceptance of being beautiful, caring, lovely, clever, you are calling them a liar and thinking them stupid for loving you.

If you have any trouble with this, visit an old people's home and ask elderly folks about how they were when they were young and realise that when you are eighty you will love your vibrant hair and glowing complexion and bright eyes and think how silly you are that your nose is not quite right or your tummy a little flabby, or whatever else you might think right now.

You will know that you have passed this trial when:

You can say these things on the list aloud to yourself whilst looking into the mirror and honestly know them to be true on every level of your being – without them being followed by, 'yes, but'. You smile and say thank you, or that's very nice of you, or whatever your phrasing is when you are complimented and honestly evaluate it rather than dismiss or become embarrassed. You welcome compliments and shirk off insults, knowing that the good stuff outweighs anything else anyway and nobody is perfect.

THIS TRIAL'S TIPS AND TRICKS

Strange things can happen when you look into the mirror. All of a sudden all that stuff that was going on inside your head is literally reflected straight back at you. There is another thing you can do too, which will amaze you.

Stand in front of the mirror and look deeply into your eyes and be fascinated. It is as if you are seeing yourself for the first time – look nowhere else for this one, just into your eyes. After a while imagine that you are looking at someone else and 'will' them to come closer, come closer, come closer. You will feel yourself physically compelled towards the mirror.

Now repeat over and over and over again, 'go back, go back, go back' and physically feel yourself moving backward.

Another interesting thing you can do with affirmations is to use the same phrase in the first, second and third person and notice the difference in feeling such as:

I am clever

You are clever

Jennie is clever

Replace my name with yours of course! Another extremely interesting thing to do is, if you have an issue with another person and often think of them negatively (with good justifiable reasons most probably because of how they have treated you badly) then, looking into the mirror, talk about them the way you would wish them to be, beginning with yourself, such as:

I am very understanding

You are very understanding

Frank is very understanding

We are very understanding

I understand

You understand

We understand.

TRIAL NINE THE AMAZING PHRASING TRIAL

"Yeah, but, nothing: can't or WON'T?"

What to Do

Throughout the day, hourly, make a note of common phrases you use throughout the day. Look at the list of your usual phrases and examine for negative aspects and rewrite them positively.

Why to Do It

Many people when asked to state their goal(s) will use language which can be evaluated as a lack of commitment to change.

Looking carefully at the phrases you use such as, 'I'll try', I'll give it a go', 'yes, but', 'maybe', 'that would be nice but in the *real* world', means you can clean up your language and clean up your vibration. Your inner self takes you literally and is always noting what you say you want for yourself. If you say, for example, that you want to win the lottery, but follow it with a smile and say that it is not likely to happen, then it probably won't.

How to Do It

Look out for these phrases that follow, in your own language patterns. Some can be regarded as 'distancing language', like 'well, it's alright for some', that is, setting you and the things you want far apart from each other. Others can be regarded as weak or negative.

You will know that you have passed this trial when:

You have written down phrases that you often use which create a negative reality for yourself and you have replaced these words with more positive phrasing. Your new phrases become a mantra you repeat in your head and out loud in the mirror. If you have done this correctly, you will hear those phrases more and more. When someone absently tells you it is a miserable day, for example, you just say it's a wet day which need not dictate your mood.

Let me just explain what will go wrong when

One of the most common was of phrasing things that you will hear as soon as you are attuned to it is that one 'must not forget'.   Hear people around you, though also yourself, say, things like 'Oh, I mustn't forget to send that letter tomorrow/go to the bank at lunchtime/pay that bill else I shall be cut off/pick my keys up as I leave/phone Mary about those tickets/pick up the kids'.

People are so imaginative that when their creativity is not applied (maybe they feel they are in a boring job and have no hobbies so there is no outlet, there are many reasons) they funnel it into conversation exchanges with you. However, these are not true conversations. These are the worried meanderings of what will happen if THEY FORGET to do something.

It is often a plea for your assistance, because in telling you about it you incur some responsibility in the whole event. 'I TOLD you that would happen' really means, 'Why did you not remind me, you were in on this too!'

The hypnotically interesting thing taking place here is that when a person says they must not forget or you see a message that tells you 'don't forget' your creative mind does not notice the negative 'don't' and it focuses on what is left. It focuses on forgetting and wonders how things will be WHEN you forget and imagines all the dire consequences of forgetting. This is how we attempt to help ourselves remember and it is ineffectual.

SO, the next time you hear 'Don't forget...' say 'Remember' and choose to correct people, for your own sake. You will notice straight away that this stops the barrage of the imaginary account of what would have gone wrong in the forgetting episode and some might even plough through with it anyway as their focus is so strong on protecting themselves in this way. For the most part though, folks tend to stop and look at you strangely. So that's just an example.

By the way, if you really want a toddler to run on the way to school etc, just tell them, as many do, 'Don't you DARE run' 'It's really important when we get there that you DON'T RUN, okay?' See what happens.

The Yeah, But Fairy

So in saying positive things aloud to yourself, or others, sometimes we inadvertently add on something negative at the end which dispels its power, such as "Oh, I would love to win the lottery but that's not likely to happen is it, though it would be nice."

Can you now understand why you yourself would reply to a compliment with a 'put down' for example, "Oh, that's a beautiful car you are driving", "Yes, but it is getting quite old now and we can't afford a new one just yet."

How about "I have a beautiful face"? Does that elicit thoughts such as 'but look at my nose and there's a wrinkle I have not noticed before, or yes, but I used to have such great hair', etc.

The Yeah, But Fairy can be your new best friend as she points out where you need to do the work. I set you this trial because YOU say mean things to yourself and your circumstances all the time and the most effective way to know what you really think about yourself and your accomplishments is to write down and examine what goes on in your head.

This is what the Yeah, But Fairy sounds like.

"Yeah, but look at this. Yeah, but it was not very expensive, I got it in the sale. Yeah, but you should've seen me when I got up this morning. Yeah, but I had a lot of help with that,…" etc.

These phrases may seem familiar though I am sure you have your own when you really think about it. So look out for the Yeah But Fairy.

Replace Yeah, but, with AND. "Yes, AND I got it in the sale, which is even better." "Yes AND when I got up this morning I made a big effort to look good, thank you!" "Yes, AND I had a lot of help with that too, which was most welcome."

Contrasts

It is a quirk of the human mind to think in contrast, to compare, to evaluate against a scale. Recognise that as soon as you think of a particular extreme, you have a tendency to think of its polar opposite.

"Oh, do you like it? Well I suppose it's not bad is it?" Replace with, "Glad you like it, yes it's good isn't it?"

"Well, I would've gone for the more expensive one if I had the money, but I suppose it will do!" Replace with "Yes, there were others available though this one was just perfect for the money".

"Yes, we would've like to have stayed for two weeks, but we had to get back, you know how it is". Replace with "Yes, one week suited us just fine, we've really enjoyed ourselves."

Here are some others to notice too

Thought is past tense; change takes place in the present.

"Yes, I thought I would perhaps go for that promotion" Replace with "Yes, I'm going for that promotion"

Might is not non-committal; will you or won't you commit yourself to change?

"I might ask her out today." Replace with "I'm asking her out today."

Like is also somewhat non-committal; will you translate that into a 'want' and a take action?

"I would like to give up smoking." Replace with "I am not going to smoke any more."

Try is a childish word for something a person doesn't expect to be successful; will you only try, or will you act?

"Well, anything is worth a try isn't it?" Replace with "This is something I am going to make happen. Absolutely."

A little is short of the mark and has no measure; how much will you go for...all the way?

"It would be good if my diet improved a little, yes." Replace with "I am making improvements to my diet every day."

Progress is not arriving; will you merely travel, or will you commit yourself to arrive at your goal?

"I am progressing steadily towards that, yes" Replace with "I am achieving new goals every day and it just gets better and better."

Why and **reasons** are either a demand for an excuse or a quest for abstract answers; do you want to change?

"I've been thinking about why this is so important to me and wondering why I think I need to change my job at all really." Replace with "This is really important to me and I know it is time for change."

Can't is a plea to be released from responsibility; Substitute "won't" and discover what stops you or how you decide not to.

"I would go to the Gym after work, but I just can't, you know?" Replace with "I am going to the Gym after work, no matter what."

More is a smoke screen and a hedge; is your goal to be confident? how will you be/behave when you are confident? Where do you want to be confident and what will happen then?

"I would like to have more money and be more valued at work and if I was more confident then maybe I could." Replace with "I feel confident to be valued more at work now and I am going to ask for a raise."

Not is not a goal and can tie you up in knots

"Well, I would say I am not as slim as I would like to be, of course. It really is not that simple, if only." Replace with "Yes I want to be leaner, stronger and healthier and I know the improvements I want to make right now."

Many problems is a way to create a log-jam so you won't solve a single one; what single outcome will you select for yourself to be committed to?

"Well, there are many problems to be addressed before I can even think about making time to do that." Replace with "I know what needs to be done now and I am going to take the time to do it."

Two BIG Reasons Why Positivity and Affirmations Don't Work For You

You will be doing some affirmations properly in the next chapter, oh yes you will! Some folks work with affirmations, standing in front of the mirror or with friends or screaming from tops of mountains to tell the Universe what they want, when the other 99% of the time, affirming quite the opposite. For example, saying aloud to yourself 'I am rich' repeatedly to attract riches to your life will not happen if:

Repeatedly, without passion!

1. It is said without the passion and driving force of the emotion of abundance, which is what FUELS the vibration and sends it spinning at the right frequency.

2. You say it ten times a day which is you think is great, when a hundred times a day you think of lack, such as when a bill arrives and you worry there is not enough in your account, or a friend asks to borrow money and you just can't do it, or you want a new car and talk yourself out of it as you can't afford it.

TRIAL TEN: CONFIRMING AFFIRMING TRIAL

"You're your own worst enemy!"

What to Do

Examine your everyday affirmations, reinforcing positive and reframing negative.

Why to Do It

I suggest that up until now you have not really known how you regard yourself. The opportunities for growth dwell within that negative that you would prefer to ignore. When you give yourself credit for what you have achieved and who you have become you begin to recognise how to achieve more and become more. Also, the criticisms and insults and things that were wrong, though were said to you that you allowed to seep into your mind by not even silently challenging, continue to chip away at your self confidence as your inner self, like a hurt child, continually asks if they were all true.

How to Do It

You have some damage to undo. This is linked somewhat to the previous chapter, so it's good you passed that trial first, though this time it is personal. Take a good look at the examples on this list (and add your own) and truly contemplate the meaning and impact on you. Find your own affirmations and which ones are helping and which are hindering. Ask yourself, with each one, a) is it true? and b) is it useful for me to continue to think this way? c) what shall I change this to? The most effective affirmations are your own positive antidotes to the negative you already use, so first you have to find them, do not use the affirmations of others, create your own antidotes. I offer examples to start you off.

I am not good enough
[maybe change to I am maybe not as *rich/slim/healthy/loved/clever* as I want to be, though I am getting there and I AM GOOD ENOUGH RIGHT NOW, BECOMING MORE, THOUGH GOOD ENOUGH, NOW]

I never have enough time
[maybe change to we all have the same 24 hours in a day and I choose to spend mine in the ways I do for the reasons I explain to myself, I AM CHOOSING HOW TO SPEND MY TIME]

It's all work and no play
[maybe change to it is important for me to enjoy life more and I AM SEEKING NEW WAYS TO RELAX AND PLAY MORE

I never seem to do anything right
[maybe change to I notice that I am focusing on things that have not gone as I would've wanted them to and I CHOOSE TO REALISE RIGHT NOW THAT OFTEN THINGS GO RIGHT FOR ME]

Everyone is just out for themselves
[maybe change to I am noticing others who are looking out for themselves more than I do and they are faring better than me, whilst I know I don't want to be just like them maybe I FOCUS ON LOOKING AFTER MYSELF A LITTLE MORE NOW]

The above is just a sample of affirmations exchanged with others every day that can affect our vibration positively or negatively and it is time to find some that help you.

You will know that you have passed this trial when:

You have a certain set of phrases that you repeat to yourself that energise and lift you and bring about a change of state to more positive awareness.   You know your perceptions are changing.

THE RESISTANCES

The resistances are emotional states that manifest inside of you. ... The TRADITIONAL RESISTANCES are often hidden within the well worn phrases that you may find that you use because you agree with them or they have passed by your consciousness and you have defaulted into using them because those around you have showered you with them. These are examples such as these:

Better the devil you know

Out of the frying pan and into the fire

It's alright for some!

You don't know what you have until it is lost

He/she's a chip off the old block

A leopard never changes his spots

Language is full of such clichés, though watch out for them emanating from your own lips because each time you repeat one you are affirming or reaffirming with another, that this is what is normal and usual for you and for life and for everything. Not all clichés are negative or harmful, though some are and these well worn phrases can be affirming your resistance to change and the dangers of moving forward. Have a good look at the small list above and write down others that come to mind and really begin to contemplate them now. These few in particular provide a strange sense of comfort in staying stuck and distance us from using the accumulated momentum which is attempting to push us forward. Now in the last chapter we spoke about other people offering such phrases though now it is time to notice how these resistances have become your own thought processes.

The phrase of this chapter, that 'you are your own worst enemy' is useful when you recognise that you have a conscious and an unconscious part to your mind and there is some part of you that seems to be your saboteur. This part wants you to stay put, to not change and cloaks itself as your protector, though it is not your friend.

Traditional Resistances

You have been taught, conditioned (there is a difference between the two), manipulated, or threatened out of receiving.

Consider phrases such as:

Pride always comes before a fall

The higher you climb the greater the fall

Self praise is no recommendation

Some of these advisories or similar were instilled into us to keep us safe, encourage us to behave, not to speak up against teachers and not to get too big for our boots which is all part of our growth and interacting with society and this is not to say that there is anything vastly wrong here. It is when we use the same phrasings to offer excuses to ourselves to stop trying and cease moving forward with our collected momentum that they can be harmful.

You were taught, conditioned, manipulated, or threatened into believing that to receive is weak, greedy, and selfish; that it is just messing with your mind. It is time to redefine. The nature of people is generally one of giving. We enjoy helping others, it is our nature to share and to want to associate with like minded folks and to give and to receive in a good natured way. When lack and shortage and not enough is perceived however, when forces beyond us conspire to persuade us that we do not have enough, are not good enough, that we need to buy this or that and that there is a limited supply and others will surely think badly of us if we do not quickly get this product, then we are thrown off balance. Our own guidance system is replaced by wanting to do the right thing and be respected and earn worthiness and deserve a prominent place in society.

Receiving versus Resisting

Think of all the things that happen without your effort! The beating of your heart, spinning of the earth, grass growing up all over the place, even weeds through tough tarmac and mold in your bathroom. So much happens without your interference and it is often our negative interference that halts our wellbeing.

WHERE IS THE PERSISTANT RESISTANCE?

What's the matter? What's going wrong in your reality?

Most problems are based on fear.   It is the root emotion of all the lesser ones we cloak it in, for example, anxiety, worry, depression, stress and many, many more.

How your negative ego blocks you

Resistance is held by the negative ego.   Your negative ego, which intervenes and blocks your manifesting much more than you are aware of and is NOT your friend, is not very clever.

When you have to think about things more deeply, look for hidden meanings, ponder on ambiguities and then have your penny dropping moments of true realisation, then the learnings are far more impactful and durable. This is why your Higher Self talks in whispers rather than loud demands of sabotage.

This is why your Higher Self cloaks meanings in metaphor, to bypass the negative ego.

I'M RICH I'M RICH, I'M NOT I'M NOT!

SO, catch yourself THINKING! If you think 'I never have enough' (money) then put yourself in the vibe of having enough and send out a genuine thought about what you have enough of, avoiding the money focus. The important thing here is to never think your negative affirmation is a terrible thing for in fact it is a gift; it is highlighting an opportunity for growth and expansion and pointing you in the direction of positive change.

You may not have enough money so to lie to yourself to try and fool some part of the Universe to take pity on you will NOT work.   However, send out the vibe of having enough love, enough air to breath, enough clothes to wear, enough water to drink and the vibe of 'enough' goes out to the Universe, attracting 'enough' back where the perceived lack is. Nature abhors a vaccum, so leave it up to the Universe to fill the void, that's not your job.

Think poor?   = being poor so .....Think rich! In what ways do you experience wealth?

Think unloved? = being unloved so..... Think loved! How are you loved and how are you loving?

Think stupid? = being stupid so.......Think wise! Hoe does your cleverness manifest?

Think ugly? = being ugly so.......Think beautiful! Where is the beauty in your life?

Think powerless? = being powerless so......Think powerful! Where is the power for you?

Write these things down in your journal diary. For this is where your work is to be done. Everyday.

TRIAL ELEVEN: 5 MINUTES TO FLIP IT TRIAL

"Come and rub shoulders with me, so some of that rubs off!"

What to Do

Working with THE PRESENCE OF ESSENCE actively seek out specifically why you want what you want and spend five minutes today, when you get up and before you go to bed to write down the ESSENCE of what you want.

Why to Do It

By figuring out what change you really want in your experience and positively interacting with the ESSENCE of it, you draw more and more similar experience towards you. In disliking someone's harsh comments to their children, you return to your own harsh treatments of the past. The fire spreads. It is so EASY to do this it works against you most of the time. When something happens and you are unhappy, your unhappy past experiences flood to mind and increase.   In other words, if you think you hate your job you will not only hate your job, you will hate your world; if you think you are unloved you will be unloved and you begin to be unloving. If you want to be rich you may avoid all those rich folks who could tell you how to become rich! You have five minutes to turn this around. Time to flip it.

How to Do It

Fully associate and immerse yourself in aspects of the thing that you want that you have access to already.   Find the essence in what it is you want and bask in it.   You want to swim in tropical waters – why? If the essence is to feel the warm water cascading over your body and your muscles relax and give in to the soothing flow and feel all the tension just leave your body, then close your eyes and stand under the warm shower and work with the ESSENCE of that which you want that you already have access to.

You will know that you have passed this trial when:

You feel closer to that which you want as you can imagine more clearly how you will feel in the having of it. You can associate with the feelings of that which you want and feel that it is more possible for it to manifest in your life. Then you are freer of your limitations of lack and have more belief that what you want is closer to you. Your vibration will have changed and you will feel that your situation is changing even though there is no clear evidence as yet in your reality. Ultimately, you will know when you have passed this trial when you have truly felt the essence of what you want to create.

THIS TRIAL'S TIPS AND TRICKS

An Example of a problem
What? You dislike the job you have currently.

Why? It bores you silly, though you are busy and you yearn to do other things with the time you spend there, which drags so much. You just know you could be so creative doing something else. Everyone else seems bored too. You count the hours until home time.

The more you think about work, the more tired and miserable you become.

An Example of a solution
In understanding that you dislike your job you will seek to be with like-minded co-workers who also dislike their job, amplifying your angst.

The solution will be to seek out those who seem to enjoy their work and spend time understanding their situation.   Remembering there was a time when you DID enjoy the work, within your current role, you use your creativity to seek out what interests you and you do things in a new way and create something that involves all of your attention easily, so much so that the time passes without you realising it.   You find things to focus upon that energise you and lifts your mood.

The Explanation
In the above example, the reasons for wanting the change of job were to express creativity, have more fun and interest and enjoy interacting and being in an environment. The worker had forgotten how to do

this and needed to be reconnected with the essence of it. Sometimes we need to see a situation through a different lens rather than allowing our beliefs (which may have originated from a disgruntled colleague) to weigh down our vibration. The way to move beyond a current situation is to take all the learnings from it and take control of one's own mood rather than being governed and controlled by the environment.

If a person wants to leave a job because they dislike a particular colleague then, surely enough, the same character tends to pop up in the next job in a different guise, if there is still something to learn from that situation.   Find something to like or admire about that colleague or a new way to get along and suddenly you may be moved to a different job.

THE FOCUS FIVE CHALLENGE

For your manifesting to work you need not to believe that it is on its way and coming, but to associate positive feelings and appropriate sensory information appropriate to the thing you wish to attract.

If you want a more exciting relationship, job, holiday, living environment, then do whatever you can to generate those feelings, to give yourself the essence of that improved state, within the same situation. If you feel this is in any way impossible, seek out the feelings you wish to experience elsewhere and overlay them on the current situation. For example, you may want a delicious meal at a top restaurant, so act as if you have that already. You may want a new car, so treat this one you have as if it were brand new. What would that be like?

Imagine, pretend, that this is already yours in some alternate universe and notice and understand what it truly feels like.

Recognise that you have little excitement about the stuff you already have, you kind of take it for granted and move on to the next thing you want, so really REALLY understand what the vibe feels like of ownership. Step into appreciation of that which you have already created and yet have lost the feeling of appreciation and reignite it.

Working with Essence

Example: you want a sports car. So look at the reasons why you want it and you will maybe descend into negativity, either talking of the lack of a vehicle you would like or the inadequacies of the vehicle you have.

These reasons are important. So, if the car you have does not have enough pull and is unreliable, you want to associate with powerful performance and reliability.

So, in this example, rather than bemoaning the absence of powerful performance and reliability, which your car will be reminding you of every time you use it and thus perpetuating the influence, seek out where in your life you have such qualities.

Every aspect of life already exists and you have more access to it than you think. You may want powerful performance and reliability wrapped up in a lovely sports car, though look for where it ALREADY is.

Remember Resisting or Receiving

Receive. Learn. Remember how. Just let it be. If we were to stop the negative thoughts about the stuff that we want it would more naturally flow to us. So let's stop. How? By being aware, by using the polar opposite of your negative thoughts, by reading this book again!

So, Where's My Sports Car?

Your powerful performance may be in that Food Mixer you have in the cupboard that was bought for you a while back that you never use, because you can always just beat eggs with a fork, can't you?

That reliability may be in that friend of yours that you can always rely upon and have long since failed to appreciate and maybe won't appreciate fully until they are no longer there.

Make a list, of where you notice powerful performance and reliability.

How about the sea? How powerful is a waterfall and how reliable is a sunrise? Actively seek out powerful performance and reliability and overlay these aspects on your car. Imagine.

What Serves You?

Some folks go and test drive the car they REALLY want and if it serves you well to do that, if it inspires you and fires you up and makes the having of it seem increasingly possible, go do it, I say. Though if it serves to make you despondent in a kind of 'I shall never be able to afford such a beautiful thing on MY salary' then stay away!

Though, if you stare in awe and wonder of the magnificence of a graceful, elegant, powerful Jaguar stalking its prey on a nature TV show and appreciate its beauty and power and you just KNOW that they can reliably use everything that they possess to fire up those muscles and power up those legs to sprint off at speed into the distance of the landscape and win their prize, then, you've got the point. There is a reason why cars are called after such animals, isn't there? There are reasons why commercials use what exists naturally in nature to sell you stuff, even down to billowing sheets of washing drying on the glorious mountain tops of the Austrian Tyrol to give you the idea that when you remove your underwear from the tumble drier in your flat that yours will smell like they do, provided you have indeed purchased the stated fabric conditioner, that is.

TRIAL TWELVE: THE HIGH VIBES TRIAL

"There's no such word as can't, aim for higher than the note and you will get there!"

What to Do

Feel Happier. It used to be easy, make it so again. Seek out happiness now.

Why to Do It

When you feel 'down' and let yourself feel your lethargy then your vibration (which, remember, is the energy signature you give off and how you attract 'like' stuff to you) loses power and you attract more of the same. Be aware that when you are feeling sad the LAST thing you will want to do is seek out feeling better, that's the law of attraction in action for you! In having a mechanism to feel less sad and more glad more often, your vibration changes and life changes to a more positive state.

How to Do It

Catch yourself feeling good, or seek out good feelings and feel your increased energy. Recognise, I mean REALLY notice, physically, mentally, emotionally and spiritually, that you actually feel lifted, energised and more enthusiastic and active, more ALIVE when you feel happy. Get happy. You have a mechanism that works for you, that actively lifts your mood. You allow yourself the time and energy to experience the many emotions you are here to experience and you bounce back quicker than before, recognising the value of the learnings within them. You realise that it is in the trying to ignore one's emotional state and pretending you feel otherwise that causes problems and that no one is happy all of the time. You recognise that one cannot experience two opposing states at any time and that once you recognise your 'bad' mood and admit it, you can switch to taking the learnings from it and focus on what to do to get back to happy.

You will know that you have passed this trial when:

Most of the day you are happy.

THIS TRIAL'S TIPS AND TRICKS

Is Happy Easy?

Wouldn't it be good to work towards being happy REGARDLESS of factors around you that used to pull you down? It would perhaps be nice to have a button, a control button for the state of happiness so that we would no longer have to work on feeling good and manifesting the good stuff, it would naturally and easily happen, if only we had a button.

Really feel what would be different in you and around you when this thing that you want manifests, and/or when this happiness 'happens'. Rehearse your happiness, appreciate what is. Know that anything is possible, so how would others react? Write all this down so you can compare when it materialises. If a new relationship will make you happy, great, if a cream cake will make you happy, fabulous, if being healthier will do it, marvellous. No one and nothing has the power to MAKE you happy, this is a job you have to do for yourself. It has often just happened for you naturally, being a resultant state by your relationship with what has been presented to you. Now it is time to switch things around, because you are practising being a CONSCIOUS creator, so your task and your trial is to feel the happiness before the changed circumstance manifests. This is how you gain control of your reality.

You are having a laugh!

When was the last time you had a good old belly laugh? Well, no matter how you are feeling right now it is time to find that laughter again and to anchor it so that you can access that state again.

Now, before you say that it is not appropriate to switch your happiness button on at work because you work in the sombre environment of a funeral parlour, let me explain about opposing states.

You have read that one cannot experience two opposing states at the same time. Often, though, we have been swept up in someone else's vibration through social media, the news reports, our compassionate response to a friend's dilemma that we can do nothing about, or even just the weather. There is a place and time and appropriateness for everything and this is not to discount or change your levels of compassion about elements of your world.

However, if you cannot sleep for worry about devastating floods and the suffering of others, or find yourself shedding a tear over a particularly sad movie you watched days' ago, or constantly in turmoil because someone you love needs money that you want to give but cannot source – then you would be advised to lift your resonance and energise your vibration because your Higher Self **now has no access to you.**

When you are down in the doldrums you will not get that inspired idea that can help the situation you are focussed upon. When you remove that focus and lift your mood, just like trying to add up some figures and the totals do not tally, when you give up on your calculations and pop to the bathroom and return, bingo, the solution to the problem suddenly seems apparent.

So. When was the last time you had a good laugh? What you need here is a mechanism for dispelling the darkness of a mood, though when you are in the black mood you will not have a way out unless you can set it up now.

Go find the funniest thing in the world for you right now. A hilarious, yes hilarious, video of animals doing crazy things, or a song or limerick or joke that has you burst out laughing.   You could even just listen to 'The Laughing Policeman' if you are aware of this or by watching other people in hysterics you cannot help but smile.

Whatever you have found (we are all different and you know what has the potential to work for you) set it up – prepare to laugh your socks off and go for it. In the height of your laugher create a button – hold your sides in a particular way or put your hand on your stomach, turn a ring on your finger around three

times, pinch your ear.   What you are doing now IN
THE MIDST OF THE LAUGHTER is creating an
anchor so that your body anchors the state of
happiness and the state will be initiated by your
'switch' or 'button'.

Now, you have to build this up. Some people slap
their thigh repeatedly when they are struggling for
breath as they are laughing so much, some fold their
arms across their chest in an attempt to stop their
body staking so much from the laughter.

This may seem extreme – and it is. Extreme
sadness needs extreme remedies and the Universe
will see to it that you have access to such stimuli
when you make up your mind to find it.   This is
exactly why when you were a child and told to
prepare for sombre church gatherings or to not 'play
up' at a strict aunt's house, you just knew there was
soon going to be something incredibly funny that you
would have to force yourself to try and stop giggling
at.

When the tide turns and now you are practising doing
the opposite.

It may be that you do not do this service for yourself right now, though instead catch yourself suddenly laughing uncontrollably at something a friend tells you soon, or even a commercial on the television. Grab it, use it, anchor it, do something to remind your body how this state feels.

Now. When you are in a neutral kind of a state, fire off that anchor, press the button, flick the switch and feel your mood and your energy heighten. Just as 'misery loves company' because of the action of Law of Attraction, then so does happiness. As your thoughts of being happy increase they will attach to others that have happened before and soon you will be reminiscing with others and reminding them to feel good too.

This is a valuable tool to use when you are in a low state. Fire your anchor and whilst you will not have that belly laugh THEN, you cannot experience two opposing states at any one time, so your low state will neutralise and you will be out of the hole.

RESONANCE EQUALS REALITY

How can I feel happy about something I want when I don't have it to see, touch, hear, feel, smell, taste right now!

Spaced Out

What separates you from that which you want is time and space.

Replace time with intensity. You may not have had something for a long time, such as that moment you were proposed to, or that time you won the raffle, or the moment your team won. You know the defining moments of your life and the intensity, the height, the peak of joy.

Forget space and create closeness. Be intimate with the essence of what you think this object, experience, or person, will bring you. Find ways to make yourself vibrate at the same level as that which you want by choosing experiences, feelings and thoughts that resonate on the same level. For example you want

to be abundant about money, so FEEL your
abundance about health.

The Vibrational Scale

Where are you on a scale of 1-10 of feeling good?
10 means feeling the best, most positive, hopeful and
expectant of good fortune you have ever
experienced. You wake up at a certain level and as
the day progresses you either hold, lift or decline.

Realising your resonance is imperative to shifting
focus, to shifting up the scale, to shifting your reality
into your most optimum of futures.

THE HIGHS AND THE LOWS

We use the terminology in our language of feeling
high when happy and low when sad.   The frequency
differs; our energy output differs according to mood.

Remember now having an experience where there is absolutely no good reason why you should be tired and lethargic; you have had enough sleep, eaten enough food etc though feel quite tired and fed up.

Then, something happened, either 'good' or 'bad' that heightened your mood, made you have to respond to life with more energy and hey presto your mood lifted and you gained access to more energy.

Raising your Resonance

So, where are you on a scale of 1-10 of feeling good then, right now? You know it is constantly changing, but right now, where are you?

It takes work though and this is where the difficulties can be. Knowing you are in a bad mood how do you acknowledge that (because when folks tell you, you will tell them they are mistaken because you are FINE!) and how do you go about lifting yourself out?

Maybe you have been relying on someone else to raise you out of it? That may have worked really well when they were in a good mood and all of their focus was on you and wanting to cheer you up.

When someone holds you as their object of attention when they are in a bad mood or when they just don't have the energy within them to shower upon you to lift you out, you can feel hurt or resentful or think the magic has gone out of the relationship, when in fact it is a lot to ask of them to continually be a in a good mood and to help you up continually.

No one is suggesting you continually stay at the upper end of the scale, because that is not maintainable and you are meant to experience the full range of the highs and lows of emotion. This is your guidance system and motivates you to move in the direction of growth and wellbeing.

Problems occur when we do not acknowledge, when we pretend, when we suffer in silence and foster anger and resentment. That is not what we are talking about here.

The ability to acknowledge your level of happiness and sadness at any one time and to deal with it, not blaming others for putting you there and being aware of the formula for plotting your escape, is part of your spiritual growth.

Likewise, attempting to save everyone else from the full range of their experience by trying to control others and events so that they are unduly protected is a huge responsibility to carry too and ultimately proves ineffective.

Know Thyself

Fostering the ability to cheer oneself up and shrug off negative vibes is a challenge, there is no doubt, though it is also a gift you can carry a lifetime and share with others.   Remember though, what you enjoy may not be what others like! We are only dealing with you here. Repeat after me, 'me, me, me!'.

This means you have to know yourself pretty well and what makes you tick.   Know what makes you laugh. You must know that when you get yourself into a bad mood you usually resist feeling better. Remember that phrase folks use when they are in a miserable mood and someone tries to cheer them up? "Oh, you are just trying to make me feel better!" Yes! Of course they are, though it's often the case that we want to stay exactly where we are, right down in the doldrums.

Are you Visual?

Find out what works for you. Find and create pictures that lift your spirits and give you energy. What pictures are in your head when you think of certain things, like wealth?   Make them positive.

Oh, by the way, when you need it most you will be resonating at a lower frequency and it will not only be the last thing on your mind to look at these pictures and images, you will maybe recoil in disgust at the happiness of them, or if others present them to you, or turn on a comedy show you say things like, 'You are only trying to cheer me up!' Perhaps you even leave the room to remain in lower vibration. This is the time to test your mettle and put on that music whether you like it or not. Find out what works.

Are you Auditory?

If so, you may notice that a sad piece of music REALLY brings you down. Likewise, an upbeat, highly rhythmic piece has you dancing in the aisles of the supermarket as you just cannot help yourself. If this is you, make sure you have your happy CD or mobile device with all those upbeat tunes on there to lift you when you need it most.

Oh, by the way, remember that when you need it most you will be resonating at a lower frequency and it will not only be the last thing on your mind to do at the time, you will want to wallow in that lower vibration. Push on through and get back to happy.

Are you Anything Else?

You may enjoy being on your own, with yourself, take off to the cinema and get some alone time to cheer yourself or be happy.

You may like being really active and immerse yourself in horse riding, paragliding or mountaineering or frantic dusting so that you just don't have to THINK of anything but the matter in hand.

My way or the Highway

Just do what works for you. You have been on the planet long enough and had enough experiences now to know yourself. You are different to others and that's fine. We often join up with those who ARE different to us to explore other ways of being happy. Then, we chastise them for their frivolity in simple appreciation of an ice cream or 'stupid' joke or relaxing bath because it is not our particular way of enjoying life. So, convince them your way is better and maybe experiment with their way of loving life, it could be fun!

THE DAY OF RECKONING - REMINDERS

TRIAL ONE

You will know that you have passed this trial when:

You notice throughout the day that friends, family and work colleagues may say to you things like, 'you are quiet today'. **If NOBODY says this to you, or remarks on your changed behaviour, you have NOT passed this trial – repeat again tomorrow before moving on.**

At the end of your successful trial day you will have at least a page full of realisations about events and conversations and new perceptions on the content of your day. This will open the gateway to communicating with your Higher Self, which currently creates your reality.

In day one's trial you learned patience and understanding by closing your mouth and opening wide. You gave yourself room, a little gap, to think. You switched off your automatic people pleasing pilot and became the Observer and found that you did not have to interact as much as you thought you had to and people still carried on regardless. You opened up your awareness and now have communication flowing from your Higher Self to you.

TRIAL TWO

You will know that you have passed this trial when:

You have genuinely been interested in the statements you have heard throughout the day and you have NOT responded automatically with your own opinion or your usual emotion. You have calmly, in a matter of fact manner, stated your intention and told your world who you are, what you are doing and given others the chance to join you. If you have been successful, congratulations and move on to the next trial, if not, repeat this trial tomorrow.

In day two's trial you created a reality and normality filter system in which to sieve through reality as you are exposed to experience. You recognised you have your own particular version of reality and it suits you just fine and you allow others to live in the world that suits them too. You have learnt the influence you can exercise in your **inner** world.

TRIAL THREE

You will know that you have passed this trial when:

In your notebook you have a list of at least twenty positive aspects to your day.

In day three's trial you acquired the hocus pocus of focus – you have learnt to use your energies to focus on that which you wish to create. You are not allowing your energies to be pushed and pulled by the tide of other people's wills or the tide of environment. From trial three you have learnt the influence you can exercise in your **outer** world.

TRIAL FOUR

You will know that you have passed this trial when:

You have acknowledged the fear and you know which fear/s belongs to you and learn that your particular fear is there to serve you and keep you safe and now acknowledged, you rise above it and trust yourself to protect yourself in a new way, drawing upon all the resources that you have accumulated by living life up until now. You know you have passed this trial when you have felt the fear and have written in detail about doing the thing that you fear most and have given your story a positive outcome. Now visualise it and feel the success and relief in achievement knowing that the next time you face a situation of this sort you have a new way forward that will lead you to overcoming rather than succumbing.

From trial four you revealed fears and continue to deal with them as you have undergone a process of releasing yourself from the shackles of fear. These fears are really contrivances that do not really exist;

they are illusory.   You are continually freeing
yourself of fear during this lifetime.

TRIAL FIVE

You will know that you have passed this trial when:

You write your three stories of the defining
moments/events and how these involved others and
how they responded to, and co-created your
situation, even if you do not particularly like the
people concerned or they are no longer around for
you. You find yourself writing detail, such as what
you are wearing and what the weather was like
during these events.

**From trial five you realise that you co-create with
others** and you have your own particular version of
them and this is how the Universe responds to you.
You understand that those around you are actors in
your play and you are the director and you can begin
to allow them to help you create the world that you
want. We are often of the opinion that people are
against us though actually there are some who want

to help. Coincidences are there to help you too if your eyes are open to them.

TRIAL SIX

You will know that you have passed this trial when:

You will have a clear and detailed description of that which you wish to have created for you in your life and what you wish to experience into your future. There are varied and different possibilities of exactly how these can occur and you focus only on that which you want not on how it will come to you.

From trial six you put your order in and you know where you are and where you would like to be next, knowing there are differing versions and possibilities of yourself in the possible futures ahead. You uncovered what YOU want rather than what others want for you. This includes advertisers, the next door neighbours, your family or co-workers or boss, or television or magazine article. This is about what you truly want deep down inside and what will bring you fulfilment, inner harmony and peace. You actually created that which you wanted (such as job) though you didn't recognise this as a successful creation because it was actually what others wanted FOR you and you wanted to please them or thought that was right for you or needed the money and you thought it was the only way to get it, or did just not then have other thoughts and evidences of what other choices there were.

No matter how insane, now matter how crazy, no matter how illogical (for your Higher Self is often illogical to the conscious ego), you are being inspired to do something. You have also learnt that this is fluid and flexible and living on that desert island may just be the tonic you need right now though two weeks' later there will be something else you are inspired to work into your experience, some other desire will manifest and you find yourself all of a sudden pining for lush forests and waterfalls, or tall elegant concrete modern buildings in the city.
You are coming out of the habitual thinking that you will suddenly be inspired with how to live the whole of the rest of your life – inspiration is for right now and will change as you gain the learnings and attitudes you need from each one. Do you want to learn to shear sheep, so go to the outback of Australia and learn how to shear sheep, whatever your thing is. There may be a guy who seems obsessed with

keeping lawns immaculate that appears to be a total waste of time to you, though in five years' time he may have his own successful gardening service because it was his passion and he was compelled to create the perfect lawn for others – it was his 'thing'. Find that thing that you want, even if other people are telling you it is stupid or that it is ridiculous and why don't you just be 'normal' or be like everybody else, you are focussing now on what YOU want to do.

TRIAL SEVEN

You will know that you have passed this trial when:

You will know the importance of writing things down on waking, you will have an idea just pop into your head, you will react differently to tv shows and chance encounters. You will have a list of coincidences, inspirations and dreams and you will have recognised what you are particularly drawn to that sparks your creativity and invigorates you.

From trial seven you realised the plight of your insight and how it has continually tried to communicate with you and you did not hear. Now you have opened up a dialogue with your Higher Self – you are listening to yourself more. Rather than blocking out these inspirations and desires and preferences or treating coincidences as insignificant, you are leaping upon them intent on finding meaning within your experience. Rather than thinking your desires are whimsy or fancy or daydream, you are noting the importance of your internal guidance system and giving importance to that communication.

TRIAL EIGHT

You will know that you have passed this trial when:

You can say these things on the list aloud to yourself whilst looking into the mirror and honestly know them to be true on every level of your being – without them being followed by, 'yes, but'. You smile and say thank you, or that's very nice of you, or whatever your phrasing is when you are complimented and honestly evaluate it rather than dismiss or become embarrassed. You welcome compliments and shirk off insults, knowing that the good stuff outweighs anything else anyway and nobody is perfect.

From trial eight you evaluate compliments and criticisms by thanking them and asking for another in your own unique way. You no longer resist either though you dismiss negative comments more easily and consider positive ones more carefully and with good grace. When someone gives you a compliment, you gracefully accept it. You have realised the disservice you have given yourself in the past when compliments and positive comments have been made to you which you have discounted, argued with or completely ignored. For example, let's say someone remarks that you have really great hair. By denying the compliment or shrugging off the comment you are actually saying to yourself that you have not great hair. In completing trial nine you are accepting that you are a person with great hair, what a blessing to have such fabulous hair. You are accepting that you are a great cook, or a brilliant typist, or handyman, you are accepting that you have talents and abilities that have either been bestowed upon you or that you have gained by strategic and determined effort and have earned the right to nod and accept that these are positive aspects of yourself and thank the world for bringing to your attention something that you had taken for granted for so long. Someone says, 'wow, you have such a great voice' and you used to think well doesn't everybody, really? No, they don't.

Nobody has your voice; your voice is unique to you, special, you are a one off. You have learnt to come out of the comparative mindset and maybe you used to compare that voice with other voices to see if they were right and this could've gone the other way, thinking how much better your voice is than others and belittle their inadequacies in your mind and thank your lucky stars you have such a great voice, but you didn't. No you did not do that because you left that behaviour behind in the school yard and in fact it became a fear, in its way. You didn't want to upset anyone and cause trouble for yourself either, you wanted to be liked so even when the Universe presented you with a friend or acquaintance that had a really nasally voice or high pitched squeaky voice, or had lost their voice completely, you felt sorry for them, fearing that you might gloat and boast about your perfect tones. Appreciation is not comparative and derisory it is acceptance and thankfulness. If it is a skill and others admire it then you have the ability to share it and teach it and maybe find that the one who complimented you on it does not want it, they just want to appreciate your level of skill and let you know they admire the work you have put in to get it. They have other things to do with their lives and maybe would never want to devote their time and effort to lawnmowing anyway, but good for you.

Deny a compliment and you are actually saying the opposite to your Higher Self. You are saying the meal you cooked was worthless or that you are a rubbish cook, you are demeaning yourself and attacking your core identity, all those important things that make up who you are, your skills and abilities, your aptitudes, your beliefs, your behaviours, the environment you have given yourself access to, your children, your family. By accepting the compliment and in recognition of positive aspects of yourself, you are accepting the higher vibrations and you are allowing yourself to flourish and to firmly and truly understand what it is that you do well. You do these things SO well in fact that the rest of the world is beginning to take note and the Universe is drawing your attention to that worthiness.

In life we tend to focus on the negative and to our shortcomings though if we actually accepted the compliments we start to realise that there is actually lots of good stuff about us. The Universe is using others to bring your attention to these things.

TRIAL NINE

You will know that you have passed this trial when:

You have written down phrases that you often use which create a negative reality for yourself and you have replaced these words with more positive phrasing. Your new phrases become a mantra you repeat in your head and out loud in the mirror. IF you have done this correctly, you will hear those phrases more and more. When someone absently tells you it is a miserable day, for example, you just say it's a wet day which need not dictate your mood.

In trial nine you became amazing at phrasing, knowing that your language creates your world so if you are using negative language you are creating a negative world and if you are using positive language you are creating a positive world. You are using more positive language now and you are creating a more positive world and you have noticed by now the positive effects it has on you and on those around you. You are not just being positive about yourself, you are noting more and more positive aspects around you. Your language builds your world.

TRIAL TEN

You will know that you have passed this trial when:

You have a certain set of phrases that you repeat to yourself that energise and lift you and bring about a change of state to more positive awareness.   You know your perceptions are changing.

In trial ten by confirming and affirming aspects of yourself you have developed an understanding of the affirmations you use in everyday life which can be positive and negative. These are entirely personal, not about environment or events or any matters outside of yourself, but clues as to how you regard yourself. You found that if you caught yourself saying you are unlikely to find a new relationship at your age because of the weight you carry and you don't feel attractive any more you may have been affirming that you are too old, too fat and ugly. When you step in and question whether this is true, are you too old and too fat and too ugly for love, then you begin to consciously realise how you have been affirming negative aspects and begin to release them.

Negative affirmations are a default program running in most of us. Poverty consciousness manifests in language as something like 'I would like to buy that car but I can't afford it', whereas if you turned it around it is 'I would like to buy that car so how am I going to produce the money? What can I do now or what creative idea can I come up with to buy that car?'

The statement that you cannot afford something is only based on present and obvious circumstances. If this is a motivation from your Higher Self to achieve more in life then the desire is useful to encourage that creativity and moving on from present circumstances. Saying one cannot afford something keeps one static and gives the illusion that things will be that way forever. I really want to purchase that car and the balance in my account is insufficient for that purpose so okay how can I use my creativity in this complex matter and create a bigger balance in my account to purchase that car. What else can I offer the world. One sales approach is do not come up with ways for it not to work, come up with ways for it TO work.

You have turned around all of your negative affirmations and you are now pumping out the positive counterparts and you are now creating ways to make things happen rather than looking for ways to stop it happening and you are noticing the changes in your world.

TRIAL ELEVEN

You will know that you have passed this trial when:

You feel closer to that which you want as you can imagine more clearly how you will feel in the having of it. You can associate with the feelings of that which you want and feel that it is more possible for it to manifest in your life. Then you are freer of your limitations of lack and have more belief that what you want is closer to you. Your vibration will have changed and you will feel that your situation is changing even though there is no clear evidence as yet in your reality. Ultimately, you will know when you have passed this trial when you have truly felt the essence of what you want to create.

From trial eleven with giving yourself just five minutes to flip it you actively found the resources in something small that you already have access to in order to change the vibration of what you are giving out, giving you more access to the bigger thing. Instead of acknowledging the lack of something you seek out the presence of the essence of it. You have access to power and reliability so you attract powerful reliable tings to you by attuning to the qualities of that which you want. The actual thing that you want is an irrelevance. It is impossible to create that car that you want and it is impossible to create that job that you want but you CAN create the vibratory essence of the car that you want or the job that you want. So do not think of the nice car you want in the driveway, work with the vibratory essence of the qualities of what that car is all about for you, for example.

If someone has a bad relationship they are going to take the essence of that bad relationship and carry it in their vibration so suddenly every man is a qualifier for a bad relationship. You are already creating your bad fortune because by hoping that this man will not turn out just as bad as all the rest, this creates him being as bad as all the rest to you - and confirms your understanding of what is real. Everyone wants certainty. Such as 'I know I hate my job, I know I don't like it but it will be there day in day out and the pay will be there week in week out and even people I do not particularly get along with will be there too because they are doing the same and there is certainty there. In fact we can all bemoan the fact that we have to work there together when we would rather be doing other things. Damn this money that I need to exchange for goods and services to keep me alive! Now I am close to hating money too!'

It is a fact that human beings generally fight against turmoil and kick and scream to keep certainty in life. Even if a person who thinks they actually hate their job or their partner - they may actually enjoy moaning about their circumstance and group together with others to complain about how certain and how futile that situation is, coming out of the discussions strangely happier than before. In being proved RIGHT there is a strange comfort and one's belief in certainty tends to bend towards negative aspects. In our formative years, as a baby and a toddler, life was exciting, dangerous, passionate and uncertain and we revelled in this, seeking to explore everything around us. Then we leant to become afraid and seek certainty so we knew how to react to life.   Time to seek certainty now in the range of possibilities and positivity that awaits.

TRIAL TWELVE

You will know that you have passed this trial when:

Most of the day you are happy.

You found in trial twelve your ability for high vibes. You found your own particular way to lift your resonance and raise your vibration. This is moving beyond just lifting yourself from a bad mood; this is acknowledging that you don't yet know just how good you COULD feel and actively seeking to raise and maintain a higher vibration. Higher vibration is higher energy levels and enthusiasm for life and passion for living. You took responsibility for your state of being and welfare. Sadness is an acceptance that nothing is going to change so whilst you are sad nothing can change. When you are happy you are looking forward to the future, to the wealth of possibilities which are fun and exciting and energising. With the uncertainty principle you can measure where something is in space and time or you can measure where it is going to, but you cannot do both simultaneously.

When you are sad there is no momentum, the wind is sucked from your sails and there is no movement other than this sadness which is static and seemingly everlasting. It is the negative face of focusing on the here and now as if things are going to be like this forever. So sadness is actually energy it is not a lack of energy because you are using all of your energy to keep yourself stuck in the point that you are in. Your natural tendency is to rise above and bounce back.

This is like driving an automatic car and having to keep your foot on the brake to stay still. If you would only relax your foot and take the pressure off you would trundle along quite nicely, there is really no need to fire up all cylinders and press down the turbo button on the accelerator, you may not be ready for that sort of a shock and maybe the environment around you would be thrown into turmoil by such speed. Though, if you merely removed your focus and relaxed that foot and noticed how the wildflowers were growing all by themselves without being tended to by any gardener, or how the weeds delicately and forcefully push apart the tarmac to break through the darkness you will remember that distraction is good when sad. Sometimes meditation and even a sympathetic ear is the last thing you need when you are down in the hole. Though watching a comedy show is probably the last thing you will think you could possible do because you are resonating at such a low level, though it may be exactly what you need. Maybe that irritating neighbour turning up on your doorstep just when you would rather pretend you are not in and not even answer the door is just the distraction you need to moan about something else right now.

Happiness is using all of your energy to move forward and gain momentum toward all those fantastic possibilities that are about to come your way. Sadness is about focussing on what you do not have and what you appear to have lost, whereas happiness is focusing on the potential and possibility of gain and what you already have. Trust in oneself and abilities and in others is restored.

Epilogue

Remember what you have learnt from this book and keep the trial alive because they are active anyway and you now have all the resources you need to resolve them.   All good wishes to you to connect yourself with the best possible future for you. Well done you, see you on the flipside.

With trial one you created some silence in your life, not just when you were alone and peaceful because that is just too easy – you did it in the face of the chaos and demands of everyday living and gave yourself a chance to think and to respond differently to the same circumstances, which is the true essence of change.

With trial two you began to bend your perception of reality and what is normal and real in your everyday life, thinking things have not always been this way and don't have to continue to be this way either and you freed yourself from influence from your environment more and more.

With trial three you realised what you actually have complete control over is your focus in the present moment though the world may like you to focus elsewhere, you could still be at work and focus on enjoyment or in pain and feel more relief. Your flexible focus is your malleable friend in creation.

With trial four you revealed a few home truths to yourself that perhaps it was not the world's fault that you didn't have what you wanted, perhaps underlying it all was a deep rooted fear that had not been revealed. You realised it is okay to still do things whilst having that protection in place, though it felt uncomfortable, which caused resistance to soften, as you proved to yourself how resourceful you are.

With trial five you recognised that you are not here alone. There are many others in your reality and no one can function properly without integrating with others.   You cannot have a job without a boss or a business without customers, or be a actor without a script or a bricklayer without the factory full of folks that make those bricks. We all need each other and your perception of some began to switch from foes to co-creator friends.

With trial six you actually put your order in for that which you wanted knowing that you have always been asking, so you are now conscious of how to do it properly for improved benefit.

With trial seven you realised that your insights have been blocked somewhat because you did not understand how your Higher Self was attempting communication with you and now you have ideas on how to provide more opportunity for that communication to come through.

With trial eight you recognised the necessity of accepting the reflected assessments of how well you are doing, or as we know them commonly to be, compliments. You learnt that these are valuable comments from the Universe to point out your strengths and that negative comments are just as useful as you assess their validity and discount or consider their truthfulness and usefulness.

With trial nine you cleaned up your everyday language and realised your language creates your world as your feelings about those thoughts impact on reality. It works both ways – your thoughts and feelings come from you out into the world to share with others and the thoughts and feelings of others (including advertisers and skilled marketers) come at you affecting your reality.

With trial ten you realised what you have been affirming to yourself for years and where that was not serving you, you created more positive affirmations to counter the negative effects and alter your vibration to a higher frequency.

With trial eleven you discovered that the essence of what you want is already accessible to you and you stopped distancing yourself from it by thinking how it might never come, rather, you looked for the feelings it engenders within you, realising you want this thing in order to feel better in some way, so you look to the essence of that feeling within your present environment.

With trial twelve you really understood that your feeling state is energetic – that being sad saps your energy and being happy invigorates you. Therefore you developed ways to top up those energy levels and boost your vibration and health with mechanisms to achieve and maintain a happy state more often and a switch to initiate when you so desperately need it most.

You have now completed all of the trials successfully and you are the creator of your universe, feels good doesn't it?

Thank you for reading!

Amazon reviews are really important to future writing projects for independent authors. Please leave a review for me because I would love to hear your thoughts about this book.

If you would like to receive your **FREE** preview of my next book please **email** info@hiprocom.com.

Thank you!

Printed in Poland
by Amazon Fulfillment
Poland Sp. z o.o., Wrocław